POLLYWOOD

Mackenzie Lowry

Outskirts Press, Inc.
Denver, Colorado

Pollywood
All Rights Reserved.
Copyright © 2008 Mackenzie Lowry
V2.0

Cover Art By John Marsigliano
Author Photo Taken By John Marsigliano

Outskirts Press, Inc.
http://www.outskirtspress.com

ISBN: 978-1-4327-2054-4

Outskirts Press and the "OP" logo are trademarks belonging to Outskirts Press, Inc.

PRINTED IN THE UNITED STATES OF AMERICA

My Brother Rudd Lowry

I want to dedicate this book to Rudd Lowry, the best brother on the face of the universe if the universe has a face. We fight a lot and he takes too long in the bathroom, but I love him all the same. I love to play with him when we aren't fighting, but I have to admit even fighting can sometimes be fun. It gives me exercise and makes me tougher. Rudd is only two years younger than I and we help each other a lot and teach each other new things. We have so many memories together and we went to so many places. He's even gone on Girl Scout trips and into girls bathrooms for me. We are amazing and stand up for each other. Don't make fun of him for hanging out with me and my friends as well as other girls. As said by Rudd, "I'm always around my sister and her friends and those other girls because I'm so hot!"

CHAPTER**ONE**

Hey. The name's Polly. Polly Brooks. I picked it. I actually planned out how my whole life went. Yeah that's right. I picked out my whole life. Where I was born, my name, what my career was, who was in my family, and everything that happened in my life. At the beginning, I was evil and I was on an important mission for the Devil. He gave me anything I wanted IF I completed my mission. Being evil at the time, I took the plans of my life and set off on my mission, but I took what he gave me and used it for myself. My plans had riches and great things for me. I dove down into my portal and began my life. I arrived as a ghost. Nobody could see, hear, taste, touch, or smell me. I rushed around searching for the woman I had chosen to be my Mother. When I found her, I jumped inside to be born.

Let me show you some of the plans:

Born into a wealthy family.
Lives in California.
I talk at 2 months.
I'm famous at 4 months.
I'm the best singer in the world at 2.

I start college at Princeton when I'm 5.
I graduate at 10.
I get twin sisters at 12 and they are Dory & Dora.
I start dating the most famous guy in the world.
We marry when I'm 19.
I'm rich and famous and beautiful with no children.
I stay 19 forever along with my husband.
I buy the world.
I live forever and ever in paradise.
THE END

That's what I planned, but I woke up being born in a box on a street. In a small town in the middle of New Jersey. The first conversation I hear is:

"Honey, we've got to bring her to the orphanage."

"No! We can't! She's just a baby."

"But we can't take care of her."

"When she goes to school, she'll learn. Then she will make money for the family."

"NO."

"I won't let you take her. She'll stay right here."

I looked around. There was a very young girl looking into my eyes. She looked about one or two. She kissed me on the forehead and for once, I felt something I never did before. Love.

Later on, I found that little girl was my older sister, Lanette. My name was Polly. Polly Brooks. That was the only thing that matched my plan.

CHAPTER**TWO**

I couldn't talk when I was 2 months old. I tried. Even though I knew how to talk when I was 'down there', but for some reason now, I couldn't. When I was 4 months I wasn't famous. My family was the only ones who knew my name. I didn't start college when I was five. I hadn't even really touched any books until I started kindergarten.

When I walked into my classroom, girls were wearing pretty little dresses. I was wearing baggy old jeans that used to be Lanette's.

"Why don't you go over there and play dress up?" a teacher asked pointing to some girls playing by a box filled with clothes.

I walked over and reached into the box. I pulled out a puffy pink princess dress.

"Where did you find that? I was looking all over for it!" said a girl wearing a crown, high heel shoes that were too big and a little yellow dress.

Now pay attention. This girl is going to be with me my whole life.

"It's the queen's dress. I'm the queen! You can be my ugly servant with brown hair and icky bangs! Gimme the dress!" she said. I threw it at her face. She turned around and spotted the teacher nearby and began to cry.

"She hurt me Ms. Nickel!"

"Come over here Nicole," the teacher said in a caring voice.

I got in trouble.

"Polly! Don't do that again," the teacher scolded. This teacher's name was Ms. Nickel. I called her "Ugly Pickle." Just not to her face. I called Nicole "Icky Nicky." Yes, I did call her that to her face.

That afternoon, I walked back to the box I call home. There were two large boxes that once held couches, leaning against one side of an alleyway. My parents slept there. On the other side was another box big enough to fit my sister and the few clothes she had. My parents set up a box for me, but I didn't use it for sleeping. I used it as my mini workshop. I made little dolls from trash and sold them for a dime each. Every once in a while, I would tell somebody they could have one doll free if they gave me a Wooden plank or a large stick. Over time I had built myself a small room. What I built myself was a wooden box except it held up better in bad weather conditions than a cardboard box would, and it was a little warmer.

Whenever I saved up enough money for a flower, I'd buy one. I'd spread the petals all over my floor to make it look nice. Sometimes I'd even use the petals to make dolls.

My sister was still at her public school and Mommy would be home from work soon. Daddy was always away at work trying to earn money. I only saw him on holidays and when we really needed him, like if one of us was sick.

This was right about the time when I began making and selling dolls. Nobody in my family knew. They thought I dug around looking for the supplies for my box room. I began working. Once I finished making 20 dolls, I took a plank of wood that I had and set my dolls up on it by the curb.

"Mommy! I want one of those dollies! They are pretty and recycled," I heard someone say.

"That's my little Nicky! Always thinking of the earth and others," her mom replied. Icky Nicky came up to me with her mom to buy one.

"Oh, never mind. Those dolls smell horrible! Let's go buy a Barbie," Nicky said as soon as she noticed it was me.

The next day at school, there was a new girl being bossed around by Icky Nicky.

"Hey! Stop that Icky Nicky," I told Nicky. She pushed me.

I made my meanest face and showed a fist. I walked toward her and she turned around and ran.

"Thank you. You're really nice," the girl said to me as she watched Icky Nicky run. She hugged me.

There was that weird feeling again: love. I didn't get this feeling a lot and I liked it. I guess not many people ever showed that they liked me. That girl and I became best friends. I loved her name, Arriana Rivers.

One day at school, Arey (that's what I called Arriana; Arey) asked me if I liked anyone. I never thought about that. My plan had been to date cute guys so I scanned the room.

"Ralphy!" I said. I thought Ralphy was kind of cute.

"Who do you like?" I asked.

"Sean," Arey beamed. I thought Sean was ugly, but I didn't say anything.

Icky Nicky heard our conversation. She wanted to get back at me for being nice to Arey. I had a feeling that's what was going on when I watched her walk away with an evil smile. Or I would have, but I was too young and not smart enough to realize.

Ralphy liked Icky Nicky, which meant that Icky Nicky was going to pretend to be his girl friend.

Icky Nicky walked over to Ralphy and asked him if he wanted to pretend marry her. Ralphy said yes.

ThE NeXt DaY...

Icky Nicky was standing under the big willow tree in the back telling everyone that her and Ralphy were going to 'pretend marry' at recess and 'really kiss.' She wanted everyone to come. Arey and I didn't want to come, but Icky Nicky's "bodyguard," Dana made us. Yes, Icky Nicky and Ralphy really did kiss. They called themselves 'boyfriend and girlfriend.' This was the stupidest thing I had ever seen in my life. Or, it was at the time. I laughed during the whole thing, but inside I got mad because she was only doing this to make me sad. That was the beginning of one of the many fights Icky Nicky and I had over the years.

Later on that day Dana and Arey were talking to the teacher because Arey hit Dana. Meanwhile, I sat alone drawing a picture.

"*We are way too young for this boyfriend stuff, or at least... they are. They're only like 5. Shouldn't they wait till they're at least 11?*" I thought.

Ralphy came up to me and said he wanted to play with me and be my friend. We drew pictures together. He said he wanted to be my friend and I agreed.

When school was over, Arey asked if she could come over because she already told her mom she was coming to my house today. This made me mad and also a little sad. I didn't have a house. I never told Arey that.

"I am a little mad Arey. Sad too, because I don't really have a house. I have something different," I told her.

Unfortunately, Arey thought that when I said "something different," I meant something different like a mansion. I had no choice to let her come home with me.

When Arey saw where I lived, she thought I was joking. I felt like crying.

"This isn't a joke Arey," I said softly. "I really live here."

"My sister doesn't come home for a little while and neither does my mom. I barely ever see my dad," I explained as I walked over to my box. My eyes were getting wet.

"Maybe you should go home," I suggested, my voice cracking. I felt so sad with embarrassment.

Arey was speechless, and left. She didn't know how to get home, but she must have found her way home through the police or something because I saw her at school the following day.

I sat there until Lanette came home.

"What's wrong?" she asked

"Well, my best friend found out where I live and ran away because we're poor. This sucks," I sobbed.

My sister was already starting on her homework and ignoring me. It just seemed natural for her to ask why I was crying, but she didn't really want to know why at that moment. She didn't really pay any attention to me till after she finished her homework. Then she made me feel better.

After that day, Arey never spoke to me (in a friendly way) again. I don't understand what her problem was. I don't know what happened to Ralphy, but I never saw him again. There was never any 'pretend wedding,' either. My best guess is he transferred schools.

CHAPTER**THREE**

That summer things started getting better. Daddy got another job that he was good at. He got promoted and we had enough money to rent a small house in town. I got to see my dad on Sundays and Wednesdays.

One day while I was trying to decorate my new room with the little I had, Lanette came in. I didn't tell my sister to get out because it was, after all, her room too.

"Let's celebrate! I'm taking you down to the beach with me. We will have lots of fun." Lanette said as she twirled around and fell on our bed. I shifted my weight from one foot to the other. "Which is why I don't wanna go to the beach. It doesn't look like much fun. I saw a picture once of the beach. It looked boring with a capitol D," I said.

"First of all, boring starts with B. Second, Mommy said, 'Take your sister with you! She looks like she needs some cheering up!' So I have to take you. You might meet some new friends," my sister said. I could tell she really wanted to go.

"Ok. Let's go!" I giggled.

At the beach I met a girl named Andy. She became my new best friend. We would talk about the stupid things like peanut butter and jelly or the important things like homework and our lives, but we always had fun.

I went to the beach whenever I could so I could see Andy. My sister stopped coming because she started to get very sick. I didn't know why or what was wrong with her, but I figured she'd be ok and brought her home a shell every day.

Sometimes Andy's brother would treat us to snacks at the snack bar. He was 17 so he knew about lots of "big kid stuff," that Andy and I didn't grasp. We went into the water a lot so I learned how to swim. We collected shells and suntanned. We did just about everything one could possibly do at the beach.

LaSt DaY Of SuMmer...
"Bye, Polly!" Andy said.
"Bye Andy! I'll miss you lots!" I said as we hugged.
Then I went home...
I woke up the next morning and yawned. I stretched and hopped out of bed. Lanette wasn't in bed. That was regular. Lanette usually woke up first, but she hadn't been in bed when I came home the night before either. I shrugged and opened my door. I walked across the hall to the kitchen.

"Guess what Lanette? Last night I had the funniest...," I began as I ran trough the doorway. I hesitated. I frowned and looked around. "Dream," I continued slowly. I opened the cabinet and pulled out a mini box of Cheerios. I sat at the table alone and ate. After a few minutes I walked into my parents' room.

"Mommy?" I asked. She was the only one there. My mom rolled over.

"Mommy?" I repeated getting a bit nervous.

"Your sister is," she began mumbling as she rolled around again.

"Your sister isn't here. Go walk to school alone."

I didn't ask anything. I just sighed and began walking to school.

At sChooL...

When I arrived, Icky Nicky and Arey were standing in one corner laughing. Arey was one of "them," now. The good news was Andy transferred schools and was held back because of her October birthday. Andy was in my class!! The two turned and stopped laughing when they saw me.

"Oh, look," Arey said rudely. "It's the...the...um..."

Icky Nicky finished her sentence with "Ugly, stinky person!"

I laughed and cupped my hands over my mouth. That was _the_ stupidest attempt to be mean to me, but we were in first grade. What would you expect? I tried to give them a look, but laughing stopped me from making a serious face. Andy came up behind me.

"Polly! I can't believe it," Andy began. Then she saw Icky Nick and Arey.

"That Nicky?" Andy whimpered pointing to Icky Nicky.

"Yup. And Arey," I said nodding my head towards Arey.

Andy stepped in front of me. "Will you leave her alone? It's not like you, Icky Nicky and back stabbing Arey, are any better than Polly! Polly is way better than you guys!" Andy said as she turned her head around to face me.

All the time I've known Andy, she's always been

11

the kind of person who isn't afraid to stand up for herself or her friends. Anyway, getting back to the story.

"Your clothes are trashy. Both of your clothes," Icky Nicky and Arey said laughing.

"And it's cute you wanna help your friend, but I'm the bigger and I could beat you up easy!" Nicky said still laughing.

"Actually I'm 7 and even if you were older, you wouldn't even be able to beat up a fly, poser!" Andy smiled and snapped her fingers.

"Mm Hm!" Andy said as we walked away.

I turned to look back at Arey and Icky Nicky's faces. They tried to look mad and tough, but you could tell they were scared inside.

I tried snapping my fingers, but it didn't work. Andy giggled. She read my mind when she said, "Practice more. Oh, and "poser," is another word I learned from my brother. It means someone who acts like something they're not, just to be cool or tough, I think," Andy said as we laughed together.

LaTer thAt Day...

When I arrived home I couldn't find Lanette.

"Mommy? Where's-," I began.

"Lanette is gone," my mother said sobbing as she stroked her hair. She guided me to the kitchen table and we sat down.

"Were did she go?" I asked.

"To a magical paradise."

"Is she having fun? Will she send me a card? What is the place called? When is she coming home?" I asked kind of excited.

"She went to heaven, Polly. She can't send you a card. She'll be there forever," my mother said looking into my eyes.

"Oh. Is heaven far away? I think I'll visit her when I get big," I said looking thoughtfully into space. I really didn't know where heaven was or what it was.

"You'll visit her. When you get big you're going to stay with her, but hopefully heaven is very far away for you," my mom said crying a little. I hopped out of my chair.

"Ok. I'll wait. Tell me when I'm big enough and then I'll go pack a suit case," I said smiling. I looked into my mom's eyes. "Don't cry mommy. I could take you with me when I go visit Lanette." My mom hugged me and laughed. I didn't know why. I didn't understand the loss. I went into my room and pulled crayons out of my draw. The ones Andy let me have. I started to do my coloring homework. *I'm going to tell Andy. Maybe she could come with me on the trip. She'll be excited.* I thought.

The NeXt Day...

"Well, do you want to come with me?" I asked Andy after I finished telling her a story. Andy wasn't smiling. She knew what heaven was. She didn't tell me. She probably expected that there was a reason why my mom didn't tell me.

"Um...sure. I'll ask my mom," Andy said. I couldn't tell something was wrong.

"Good," I said smiling, "Lanette will be so happy. I wonder why she didn't take all her things," Andy laughed.

"Maybe I could teach you about your religion so you know all the stuff you need to know for your communion. I mean, I'm Jewish so I don't know a lot about Christianity but I know a little. My cousin is Catholic," Andy said.

"OK," I said cheerfully. I was so excited about seeing my sister. I began twirling around. Andy laughed and began to twirl too. We laughed as we twirled our way down the block. From that day on, that's what we always did. Twirl our way down the street.

Andy and I had a lot of fun through 1st and 2nd grade. In 2nd grade Andy started to teach me a little about the Jewish religion, too.

CHAPTER**FOUR**

The EnD Of 2nd GrAde...

I had a small communion party on April 16. The same day I received my communion. Only Andy's family came, but that's OK. The parents talked while Andy and I played, and her brother, well, he was out with his friends.

"Let's go to the mall! We could buy new shoes and maybe we'll see *Ken!*" Andy said swinging a Barbie doll around and giggling.

"Ok! Ken is so cute! Maybe he'll ask me to go watch a movie at the movies!" I said.

"Not if he asks me first!"

"But he is going to ask me because I'm cute!" I said in a little squeaky voice. Andy laughed and put down the Barbie.

"Teenage girls don't say 'I'm cute' and they don't talk like that," Andy said playing with the lace on my white communion dress. It belonged to Lanette. Andy sighed. She wasn't sighing because she thought something like *Wow, Polly sure is clueless!* She was sighing because she was bored of playing Barbies.

Andy stood up and walked over to a window. She smiled.

"Polly! It stopped raining! Do you wanna go outside and I can teach you how to play baseball?" Andy asked cheerfully. She turned around to face me.

"I don't have anything to play it with." I said looking down at my white socks. I moved my feet back and forth.

"My brother does. We can walk to my house and get the stuff to play with! Besides," Andy said beginning to bat her eyelashes, "Maybe *Ken* will be there",

I laughed as she reached out and I took her hand. I asked my dad and mom if we could walk down and get the stuff and he said, "No."

As Andy and I slowly walked back to my room, moping, I heard my parents whispering. I grabbed Andy's arm. She twirled around. I put my finger to my lips and signaled her to follow me. We stood against the wall listening.

"It just isn't working," my mom said.

"Maybe you should try a marriage therapist," Andy's mom suggested as she and Andy's dad joined hands. "It worked for us."

"We already tried that," my dad said, "I didn't even know those therapists ever actually helped people. I thought they always messed up matters. She is afraid of me. When I yell, she runs out of the room in fear of me."

"That's because you threaten me," my mom said turning her face away from my father.

"I never actually did hurt you and I never actually will!" My dad said.

I turned and looked up at Andy who looked scared. We had no idea any of this was happening.

"This is weird," I whispered. I didn't know much about words like 'threaten' because I was 8, but I did know something was wrong.

"Then it's over with," my mom said. She stood up from the table. "I'm going to go check on the girls."

Andy and I looked at each other and ran into my room. We sat on my bed and looked out the window as if we had been sitting there for a while and we really wanted to go out. By this point I didn't want to go outside that badly. I wondered when and why this fighting took place. I also wondered why they would discuss this with their friends instead of just among themselves.

"How are you doing girls?" My mom asked as she walked into the room.

"Fine," Andy said. I looked at her, but I didn't turn my head. I decided to follow her lead.

"Fine. Just fine," I said. Andy turned around.

"May we'll go outside Mrs. Brooks?" Andy asked.

"Mr. Brooks said 'No'. Sorry, girls. What else would you like to do?" My mom asked. By this point I was sitting on my bed, back against the wall. I wiggled around in my spot trying to get comfortable. I looked down.

"Polly?" my mom asked coming in to sit on the bed. "Was there anything you had in mind?"

I looked up. "No," I said.

"Well, If you need my help I'm right in the kitchen, Ok?" my mom asked.

I looked closely at my mom. She was so pretty. Looked nothing like me. *Why would somebody threaten such a pretty lady?* I thought as I tilted my head to the side a little to get a better view. My mom laughed.

"My dear Polly, what on earth are you doing?" she asked.

"Nothing," I said moving my head back to where it was.

"Are you OK? You seem sad." My mother looked concerned.

"No I'm OK," I answered smiling.

CHAPTER**FIVE**

That summer the divorce papers were filed. I was spending weekends with my dad, who was working almost 24/7, and weekdays with my mom who was currently dating a kind man with a good job. My mom said, "George is kind, he has good business, and he appreciates me and the decisions I make. If we have different opinions we can work it out. This is how a REAL couple should act, Polly. Do you like him?" I said he was ok. My mom went on. "I think he's the one. Your father just wasn't the one. I think George is."

George came over for dinner one night in late summer. I invited Andy over the same night so she could help me. I liked George and if my mom couldn't be with my dad than I took the second best thing or guy.

"Hi, Polly! How are you today?" George asked giving me a kiss on the cheek. He was tall with glasses. He was bald at the top of his head and the little hair he had was black. He wasn't too thin or too fat. He wasn't muscular either. With my mom, they didn't look like a bad couple. They were an OK looking couple.

"Great! Oh, this is Andy!" I said gesturing to my friend.

"Oh pleased to meet you Andy!" George said shaking Andy's hand.

"Same here," Andy said trying her best to be polite. Andy looks like George a little in the face. He looked like he could be Andy's dad. They had the same color hair and eyes. They also had the same nose. Andy's hair was long. Down to her butt. George's wasn't. He was half bald. I already told you that.

We all sat down for dinner a little while later.

"So what's new?" George asked to no one in particular.

"Well," I began, "My mom told me she thinks you're the one."

My mom turned bright pink. George laughed. Not, like, at her. More as if I told a joke or something.

"Is that true?" he asked smiling.

"Yes," I answered stuffing broccoli into my mouth. It was my signal that it's mom's turn to talk.

"Really?" He asked my mom smiling.

"Well...I...she...yes. I guess I did," my mom said.

Andy smiled. She was clearly satisfied with watching. She was OK with not being part of the conversation.

"Well maybe I AM the one," George said cocking an eyebrow as we all laughed.

I think I helped my mom that day because two days later she was engaged to be married.

They bought a house not too far from where we were living before, but it was bigger. It actually had two floors! George made enough money to support the new family.

CHAPTER**SIX**

ThirD GrAde...

My grades were very good so far in the year. The only bad thing was that Ryan, the grossest boy in our class, liked me! Arey moved on September 21st, but Icky Nicky stayed. Dana came back this time. Icky Nicky and Dana always made fun of me. Whether it is about Ryan or just me alone. I got so mad that one day I punched Icky Nicky at recess. I had told Andy to let me go on my own this year as far as defending myself goes. Besides, she wasn't in my class. Icky Nicky didn't tell on me for punching her because I told her everyone would call her a tattletale. Even Dana because Dana was the kind of person who followed the popular girls. She didn't care who the popular girls actually were. She just followed them.

One day Icky Nicky and Dana came up to me.

"Hey Brooks!" Dana said. I continued what I was doing.

"What?" I asked.

"I just wanted to say how mean you were to Nicky the other time," Dana said slowly.

"That was the best use of words you can come up with to try to intimidate me?" I asked laughing. I learned what intimidate means from Andy's brother. When I was at Andy's house, her brother gave us vocabulary lessons, well, sometimes.

Dana's dark skin turned as pink as it could get (which wasn't really that pink).

"Well...Well...," Dana began trying to think of a comeback. She gave up and went to her seat to finish her project.

"I wanted to say thanks," Icky Nicky said looking at my project. *"Coward,"* she muttered.

"Excuse me?" I said astonished and finally looking up. I said that not only about her apologizing, but her saying 'coward'. "Really?"

"No! Of course not! I was pretending to call Dana a coward and pretending to apologize. Dana was pretending to be embarrassed. I don't know exactly why I did that, but I just felt like it," Icky Nicky said smiling. With that, she walked away. I gave her a look. Wasn't anybody besides Andy and me ever going to grow up? To me, Icky Nicky wasn't even mean anymore. Just really annoying and dumb.

After school Andy came over and brought her flower girl dress. We were the flower girls at my mom's wedding. We got changed into our dresses and admired ourselves in the mirror.

"We look fabulous! Spectacular! Incredible!" Andy said dramatically in some weird accent I never heard before. We laughed.

"Polly? Do you think George and your mom are getting married a little too early?" Andy asked.

"It's not about how long you were dating, but if you love each other which my mom and George *do* love each other." We spun around in our dresses just as we heard a knock on my bedroom door.

"Girls? Are you done yet? I'm going to take you

guys to the beauty parlor. Then I'm going to leave. Andy's mom will pick you up from there," George said.

"We're ready!" I said cheerfully as Andy and I stepped into the hallway.

"You two look beautiful!" George said as we posed for him.

Neither Andy nor I had ever been to a wedding or gotten our hair done at an expensive parlor. We were so excited.

AfTer The WedDing...

My mom and George rode away in a pretty white stretch limo to the party. The wedding was boring, but Andy and I were both happy for my mom and George.

We went into Aunt Malinda's car. Aunt Malinda was George's sister.

"Hi girls!" Aunt Malinda said.

"Hi!" we said.

"Umm.... Polly? Do you remember the name of the place that your sister...um...moved to?" Andy asked me quietly.

"No, but I'm still going to see her," I said.

"The place she went to was Heaven," Andy said quietly.

"No it wasn't. Heaven is where people go when they die," I said.

"Really! She did! Even ask your mom at the party!" Andy said looking into my eyes. She looked serious. I turned and looked out the window. "I'll ask, but only to prove you wrong."

"Your sister moved? I didn't know you had a sister!" Aunt Malinda said. Andy slapped her forehead and dragged her hand all the way down her face.

"Her sister did not move! Her sister is up there," Andy explained pointing to the roof of the car.

"I'm so sorry. I didn't know," Aunt Malinda said with a concerned voice. I just continued staring.

As soon as we arrived at the party, I ran up to my mom and asked her, " Did Lanette move or did she go to Heaven because I told Andy that Lanette moved, but she doesn't believe me."

"Who's Lanette?" George asked quietly.

"Um...Polly. Polly, Polly, Polly," my mother began. She looked sad. She looked like she was trying to hold back tears. "Lanette is still alive, but she's not alive here."

My mom kneeled down so she was at my height. "She's alive in Heaven. And you will see her again one day."

My face fell. "Oh," I said. Andy put her arm around me as we walked outside.

"Who's-," George began.

"My oldest daughter. She left us when Polly was 5 so she didn't understand what had happened to her sister," my mother said.

OuTsIdE...

"I shouldn't have told you," Andy said drying my tears.

"No. It's all right. If you hadn't told me I wouldn't have found out," I sobbed looking down at my watch. "I have to go soon. I have to go to my dad's house."

I walked inside to tell my mom that I have to leave soon, but before I reached my mom, her wavy blonde hair flowing down her shoulders and her silk dress shining from the reflection of the sun, I was overwhelmed with hugs and people saying "It's okay,

Polly!" or "I'm so sorry, Polly",

I looked up at all the people. I felt so small. They were all so tall and staring at *me*. I didn't know what to say so I just gave Andy a look that said, "HELP!"

"Um...," Andy to the rescue! "I talked to Polly outside and she said she would be fine as long as she kept the attention directed towards anyone other than herself. Like the new couple",

Everybody spread out in the room saying things like "Ok," and "What ever you say",

I hugged Andy as a horn honked outside. It was my dad. Andy went to tell him that I'd be right out.

"Mom? Dad's here I kinda need-," I couldn't finish my sentence. Mom and George hugged me. *Great, more hugs!* I thought.

"Were so sorry, Honey. I should've told you," my mom said.

"Dad's here. I gotta go," I said. Mom and George exchanged worried looks.

"Your *father* is *here*?"

"Um...yeah. I gotta go now."

"No! I mean you're supposed to stay this weekend."

"The judge said I go with him on weekends. Love you, Mom! See ya, George!" Was there something mom and George knew about that they were hiding from me? So outside I went. My mom looked nervous as she dialed a number and George took out paper and a pen. He began to stare at my dad's car and scribble something down. I wasn't worried that much.

At My DaD's HoUsE...

My dad hadn't said anything to me yet. Not even hi. There was a newspaper in the front that he was try-

25

ing to hide. When we got home I asked him if he had any plans for us this evening.

"Nothing much. I have to work," he said.

"How's Katrina?" I asked. Katrina is the one girl-friend my dad has ever had (since my mom and him got divorced) who lasted more than just one dinner or something. And I hoped this was my dad's girl and she would last longer.

"Not good," he said. It seemed like my dad was trying to keep his sentences short.

That night I couldn't sleep. I went in my dad's room trying to wake him up. His house was very small. Two bedrooms and another room that acted as a kitchen and a living room.

I saw the newspaper stuffed into a draw. I turned my head to read the outline. It said WOMEN FOUND DEAD IN TRASH BIN OUTSIDE OF NANCY'S PIZZA. I almost gasped, but I didn't want to wake my dad at this point. I was too scared. The picture on the cover was Katrina's dead body. Her neck sliced. I was tempted to read the story to find out what happened, but, out of fear, I didn't. Instead I ran into the guest room and forced myself to sleep.

The next day I tried to wake up as late as possible. I woke up around 11:00AM.

"Hey, Sleepy Head," my dad said ruffling my hair. He seemed like he was in a better mood.

"Dad? Can I read the cartoons in the part two paper?" I asked softly.

"Well, sure!" He said handing me the paper. I guess he thought that the Katrina story wasn't in the part two of the paper. I hoped it was.

"Ah Ha!" I said as I flipped through the paper and found the story on Katrina. I flipped to the cartoons so my dad wouldn't know. "Found it! Hey,

Dad, do you think I could read this in my room? I'm not feeling so hot."

"Sure. Call me if you need anything," my dad said. I walked upstairs and settled in a spot on my mattress. I began to read the Katrina story.

The cops had interviewed people at the restaurant and people who worked there. They said that a man was with the lady.

"Did this man use a credit card? If he used a credit card we could track him down to find more information about the situation," one of the cops had asked the waiter.

"No. He paid in cash," the waiter said.

One of the people said they saw the couple fighting over something, but they didn't know what. Two others said they saw the fight too.

"It wasn't an aggressive fight. Just arguments, but the man looked mad," one man had said about the incident.

The waiter said that the two went out the back door after the bill was paid. After investigating a little, the cops found a wallet in the dead women's pocket. I was right. It was Katrina.

I was more scared than I ever was before. I folded the article as small as it could go and stuffed it deep in my pocket. I shivered as I walked downstairs and placed the newspaper on the table. I looked around. He wasn't in the kitchen slash living room. I saw him in his room. I watched through the crack of the door. There was my dad inserting a needle into his arm. I knocked on the door and backed away as I heard rustling around. I figured he was trying to clean up quickly.

"Dad? You there?" I asked.

"Um...Yes. I'll be out in one second," he answered

27

opening the door and smiling.

"What do you want to do today?" I asked. "I'm feeling much better."

I actually was feeling much worse.

CHAPTER**SEVEN**

Sunday NiGhT...

"**H**i, Mommy!" I yelled running out my dad's door and racing to George's car. "Hi, George!"

They waved happily. They looked really excited. I said Good-Bye to my father before hopping into the car. We began driving. "I have some not so good news to-"

"We have excellent news to share!" George interrupted, looking into his mirror at me.

"Tell me!" I said. Mom and George looked at each other.

"I'll tell her," Mom said smiling. She turned around in the front passenger seat to face me. "We're having a baby!"

"Wow! Boy or girl?" I was so excited that I almost forgot to tell the bad news.

"We don't know yet," George said grasping my Mom's hand in his.

"Now what was that you wanted to tell us?" Mom asked.

"Oh yeah." My face fell. "Um... When you see a news story about murder and you think you know who did it, but you're afraid to say and then you see the person giving themselves a shot while not being in the doctor's office, what do you do?" I asked looking down at my feet. I moved them back and forth. All was silent except the stuttering engine. George was the one who broke the silence.

"Well...," He began glancing worried looks at my mother. "First off you should tell you parents who this someone is." George pulled up outside my favorite restaurant and looked me in the eye. I had forgotten we were going out for dinner that night.

"Um... I think that Dad killed Katrina," I said still staring down at my feet. I could tell that's what my parents had been thinking.

"Well, let's not worry about that. We'll call the police. They can take care of the situation from there. Then, I'll read the story in the news and your mother will see if you can stay with us this weekend," George said lightly touching my leg.

I hopped out of the car. I forgot all about the coming baby. We walked in to my favorite restaurant, T.G.I. Fridays, and I ordered the usual. Mac and cheese.

ThE nExT dAy...

"How's Dad?" I asked shoving a spoon full of cereal into my mouth.

"They're investigating," Mom said as George walked into the kitchen in his pajamas. "Morning, Hun," she said giving him a kiss. I giggled. George looked funny in those pajamas. The pants were to short. They only reached his knees. The shirt was too long. It went past his hands. But the best part was the picture on the pajamas. Dancing bunnies. I looked down at my own pajamas. I was wearing a T-shirt that was too big on me (so it was like a night gown) and it had Happy Bunny on it. The shirt read "Cute, but Psycho."

"Go get dressed while I make breakfast for George and myself. Remember, you still have to meet Andy on the corner," Mom said. I responded with a simple "OK," and ran up to my room to get changed.

When I got upstairs I saw a man on my roof looking down at me. I got scared and was about to head for the door when the man jumped in side lifted me up and took me away. I yelled and kicked and screamed. I heard running. It was Mom and George racing up to see what was wrong. The last thing I saw was my curtain moving. Mom and George were looking out at me. The man jumped down still holding me and punched me in the face. I blacked out.

tHe mAn'S hOuSe... I tHiNk...

I opened my eyes. I was tied to a chair blood dripping from my forehead. I felt dizzy as I stared down at my feet. I felt a tug on my hair. *OW!* I thought as my head was pulled up.

"You up, girl?" the man asked. He sounded mean.

"Yes?" I said like a question. My eyes were half shut. The last I remembered was my mom telling me to go get dressed.

"Where am I? How did I get here? Why am I here?" I started mumbling.

"You're here cuz I want money," the man said. "If you wanna, live your parents gotta pay 10,000 dollars."

"10,000 dollars?" I asked.

"Yeah."

"Why did you take me of all people?" I asked.

"You ask too many questions kid. Nothings gonna

stop me from killing you if I don't get paid."

"Can I watch TV?"

"Sure." The man tossed me a remote laughing softly. It hit me hard in the stomach and fell to the floor, but I couldn't think about that now. I don't know why I asked to watch TV, but if I were doing that, the man would be less likely to think I was planning to escape, perhaps. I whispered a little "Ow," under my breath and squeezed my eyes shut. A tear rolled down my cheek. It turned red before it reached my chin.

Ring! Ring! A phone rang. The man picked it up.

"I gots some business to take care of. You're hidden under ground and I'm locking the door from the outside. You won't be able to escape. So don't get any ideas," The man said grabbing his jacket.

I watched him carefully. I kept paying close attention till I heard the latch lock. I looked around. I was in so much pain. I saw a closet and dragged myself towards it. It was already half open. I used my foot to open it more. I looked around the closet. A bag. I tipped my chair over. I began crying as my head hit the ground. I pulled the bag to me with my teeth and searched through it as much as I could with my hands. My arms were tied so it was hard. I found a knife and began to cut the rope. When I got down to the last strings I accidentally cut my arm. I cried so much. If I found no way out, then this whole thing would have been pointless, but I had to take a chance.

When I was freed, the first thing I did was stand up and try to smile. I tried finding a way out. I saw a door. I went through it. Bathroom. There was another closet. I opened it up. There was a small window. There was my escape. I piled up all I could find in the closet till I could reach the window. I opened the latch and looked around outside before jumping out. This really was a secret underground room in the middle of a huge forest. I quickly jumped down and ran into the other room. I searched around for a compass or something. I found one. I took it and ran back into the bathroom closet. I went up to the window and climbed out. I tried to remember what side of my town that I lived in. We learned it in school. I shut my eyes and thought hard. I live in the west. Right next to a forest. Now, what side was the forest on? I thought really hard. I heard cracking leaves and quickly opened my eyes. I sighed with relief when I saw a deer. Deer. I remembered! George and Mom went for a camping trip one time. They said there was deer there. Which way was it? Oh, yes! It was west. I knew that if the forest was right next to my town, and it was farther west than my town, I should go east. I looked down at my compass and slowly turned all the way around and then followed the compass. I went east.

AbOuT 3 HoUrS later...

Just when I was about to give up, I saw a clearing with a small town. I smiled. I was so happy. I wiped a tear from my cheek and ran to a Deli. I walked in side. Everybody stared at me. I was bloody on my fore-head. And my left sleeve had turned bright red. My eyes weren't all the way open and I was barefoot. My hair was messy.

"Oh my! I must take you to the hospital right now little girl!" the lady at the counter said.

"No! I just need help," I said. I turned to face the people on line. "Is it OK if I go before you all?"

Everybody nodded or said "Yes," or "Sure," or "OK."

"Come back behind the counter young lady!" the lady said. I could tell she was worried. "Tell me what happened." I told her the whole entire story starting when my mom told me to go get changed and ending when I got to the Deli.

"And now I just want to go home," I said, crying at this point.

"Child you've been gone since yesterday. You're on the news everywhere! Every one is looking for you. I'll take you home. Here, have something to eat. I'd imagine you're hungry," the lady said holding my hand with one hand and a bag of muffins and bread in the other. I spread a weak smile across my face. The lady got somebody to take over and she took me to her car. I began eating.

At My HoUsE...

I woke up, not noticing I'd fallen asleep. The old car's engine was sputtering loudly as we pulled into my driveway. The lady opened the car door and rang my doorbell. My mom answered. She looked sad.

"Um... Your daughter came out of the forest and into my deli looking like this," she said quietly as I stepped up to the door. My mom's eyes filled with tears and she hugged me.

"Thank you Miss." My mom said pulling me inside. "Come in. Is there anything you'd like? Anything at all?"

"No thank you. I'll be on my way. I'm glad to see you're all safe and happy. Well, close to safe," the lady said.

Then she left. I hugged George and Andy who was in my house at the time.

"We are taking you to the hospital right away to be treated," George said. "Actually, your Mom will.

On the way, you tell us the story and we'll go to the police."

"Polly! I'm so happy you're back! We missed you and we didn't know where you were and-"Andy began her voice breaking. I hugged her tight. I was crying too. "I'm OK, Andy. I'm OK."

CHAPTER**EIGHT**

9 MoNtHs Later...

"**H**e's so cute!" Andy squealed as she, George, and I stood outside the emergency room looking at my new brother, Skylar John. I was healed now. I had gotten stitches on my shoulder and they treated my head, but it didn't need stitches. My dad had been sent to jail after a long trial 7 months before. So was the guy who kidnapped me.

George was practically crying at the sight of his healthy, new son.

"Summer baby," I giggled. "Little Sky."

"Little Sky. That's a good nick name!" George said.

Later, Mom let me hold the baby. "Hey, Sky!" I said smiling and looking into his eyes.

"Since you two are 9 years old now, I might let you watch Skylar. Not a lot. Just sometimes," Mom said smiling.

Andy and I leaned down at the same time and kissed Little Sky on the head. We laughed. We turned to each other and stuck our fingers down our throats and made choking sounds as George and my mom started kissing.

Andy and I were going to love playing with Little Sky.

On our way home, Andy and I talked a lot about all we were going to do with Little Sky this summer. We had bought him little flip-flops and swim shorts. We hadn't thought that the only body of water Little Sky would be going in this summer was the bathtub!

ThE fIrSt DaY oF sChOoL...

"I can't believe how boring Little Sky was!" I told Andy as we walked to school.

"Yeah!" Andy agreed. "I mean-"

"Hi!" we heard a voice say. We turned around to look.

"Hi," I said looking. There was a girl standing there looking at us.

"I'm Tina. I just moved here from L.A. I'm in 4th grade. I'll be 9 tomorrow. How old are you guys?" Tina asked.

"Same as you. No! Wait! I mean. We are already 9, but we're in 4th grade too," Andy said. Tina had blonde hair down to her shoulders. She was thin. She had blue eyes that sparkled. Andy and I looked at each other. We both thought the same thing: *Icky Nicky girl. Don't get too close.* We talked to Tina for the last two blocks that we walked and of course, as we thought, Icky Nicky jumped right to Tina.

"Hi!" Icky Nicky said right before dragging Tina away from us. Andy and I shrugged. This is what happened when Andy and I tried to make new friends.

Icky Nicky and Tina walked to the front of the room.

"This won't be good," I whispered in Andy's ear.

"The teacher just left the class for one moment so I'm in charge. This is Tina. She's new here, but she's just like all of us. Except Polly who isn't like any of us," Icky Nicky began.

37

"But," Tina began in a small, shy voice. Five minutes ago Tina was the loud chatterbox. Icky Nicky transformed her into some puppet that did what ever she said and never spoke against her. "I have a lot in common with Polly," Tina piped up. Icky Nicky narrowed her eyes at Tina and said something. I don't know what she said, but it sure did shut Tina up!

"Any way, Polly is our servant. You can make her do anything you want her to do, and she will do it," Icky Nicky said staring me down. That was the thing with Icky Nicky. She had power because people were intimidated by her.

"No I will not," I said. Icky Nicky tried to intimidate me again, but it didn't work.

"Just try," I said. I sat in my seat and began to unpack. Icky Nicky and I were mortal enemies and nothing could change that.

Andy came up and we gave each other a high five. I laughed and shook my head as Andy walked off to her class.

"Sorry, Tina. I thought we'd be good friends, but then you got infected with the Icky Nicky," I said passing Tina and Icky Nicky.

Inside Tina was scared of Icky Nicky. Neither Tina nor Icky Nicky said one word. I gave them my evil smile.

2 WeEkS lAtEr...

"Will you take your brother for a walk, Hun?" my mom asked washing dishes.

"But, Mom, I wanted to check out the new park!" I said. At the time there were only two parks that I knew of. There was a park in my town and Central Park. I wasn't talking about Central Park, but I did want to go there.

"Can't you take him with you?" My mom asked pulling out a towel and drying her hands.

"I'll be back in..," I looked down at my watch. "2 hours. I'll be back here in 2 hours and I will pick up Little Sky." I set my alarm.

"But it'll be dark then," Mom said.

"No it won't. Right now it's 11:30 Saturday morning. Not even lunchtime." I walked out the door.

I walked through the park gate. There weren't many people. I saw some people spreading out picnic blankets. I guessed they were going to eat breakfast or lunch. Or neither.

I turned and began to walk down a pathway. I saw a lot of open fields and courts. Then the path began to go through some forest. I came upon a little pond and began to toss rocks in. Suddenly, I heard cheering. I stood up and tried to look through the brush. I checked my clock. I still had an hour and half left. That was plenty time to check it out. I followed the path further.

"GO! RUN! GO HOME!" a kid on the bleachers shouted. The kid was kinda tall. About 6th grade. The other kids around him were all different ages. Some older, some younger, and some the same age. But they were all boys.

One kid slid onto a white plate near a backstop and the kids on the bleachers yelled and high-fived each other. I leaned against a tree smiling. That looked like fun. I knew it was baseball, but I had never played baseball before. The tall kid spotted me.

"Hey! Look! Who's that girl watching us?" he said.

"Can I play?" I asked walking forward.

"We don't usually let girls play. Besides our age minimum is 10," a small kid spoke up.

"I'm almost 11," I lied.

"Lets see what you can do, Little Girl," he said handing me a bat.

"The names Polly to you," I said taking the bat.

"I'm Coach Skylar to you," Skylar said. "And you're on my team."

"Oh, I have a brother named Skylar."

"Yeah and I don't know one person in this big world with the name Polly besides you. Now get out there and play!" He pushed me onto the Home plate.

Skylar walked to the middle of the field and threw the ball.

"Do you know how hard that is? You're going to hit me," I said jumping back.

He laughed as I threw him the ball. "That's the point. STRIKE ONE!"

He threw the ball again and I swung before it got to the bat. I missed.

"STRIKE TWO!" a kid on 1st base said as everyone laughed at me.

"She stinks at this!" one kid laughed.

Skylar threw the ball. I narrowed my eyes and stared. I could tell this was one I couldn't hit so I didn't swing.

"BALL ONE!" the kid behind me shouted. He was the catcher.

Skylar threw the ball once more. *I have to hit this. I have to'*, I thought, staring at the ball. It was a good pitch. I swung. Then I heard a loud crack and Skylar shouting, "RUN! RUN!"

I looked up. I hit it! I ran to 1st then stopped, but Skylar told me to keep running. I ran to 2nd, 3rd, HOME! I made it home.

"Anyone have a spare baseball?" a kid asked.

"Nice job. You're on the team," Skylar said. I expected a smile, a high five, something, but that was all I got. I could tell some people weren't happy about getting a girl on the team.

We practiced later on. I wasn't horrible at throwing, but I wasn't great either. I stunk at catching. I checked my watch. It was already 4:00!

"I gotta go!" I said.

"Game on Thursday 5:00 sharp! Buy a mitt and bring it with you!" Skylar called after me.

At HoMe...

"I was so worried! Where were you?" my mom asked as I opened the door and walked inside.

"Playing baseball. I'm sorry. I lost track of time," I said looking at Little Sky. I walked over to him.

"Sorry you missed your walk," I said. Little Sky made a face like he was laughing. For some reason, I just now realized that Little Sky didn't care about a walk. He couldn't walk anyways.

"You're grounded till Wednesday. Don't see how you could lose track of time when you had your alarm on," she said. I groaned. I had set my alarm, but I forgot to turn it on. I picked up Little Sky.

"Do you wanna go watch some stupid Barnie show with me?" I asked him. He smiled again. We went to go watch Barnie. Well, actually, more on the side of making fun of it.

At DiNnEr...

"Can we go buy a mitt tomorrow?" I asked eating my spaghetti.

"No," mom said. "Yes," George said at the same time. They looked at each other.

"No. She cannot buy a mitt. She was supposed to go to the park for two hours. Then she was supposed to take her brother for a walk. She came back about

4 hours too late. I was so worried. And Skylar never got his walk. What does she need a mitt for, anyway?"

"To play baseball," I said. "Little Sky doesn't even care about walks! He can't even walk at all yet!" I knew any other parent would let me get a mitt. They'd say," Sure! Of course I'll buy you a mitt!"

"You don't play baseball. And his name is Skylar," Mom said. Mom always got ticked when I called him Little Sky.

"Mom, I call him what I want ok? I love being with Little Sky. We always smile, but I'm on a team of boys that I met at the park. It's really fun and I'm good at it. I want to play. Everyone's nice especially Coach Skylar," I said. I lied about the Skylar part. I was still waiting for acceptance.

"Skylar? How many people are named Skylar?" George asked. Knowing it was strange to know two people with the name Skylar because it wasn't common around where we lived.

"No," Mom said ignoring George's question.

"You know what? Forget it. I'm going to my room. I'll borrow a mitt from Andy," I said pushing back my chair. *Why do we have to make a big deal about this? It's just a mitt!* I thought. I was right. It's just a mitt. I'd buy a mitt for anyone who asked unless I didn't know them. It was a small thing.

Little Sky smiled at me on my way up. I smiled then walked away. When I got into my room I heard him burst into tears. I shook my head and got ready for bed.

ThUrSdAy...

"How am I going to get out of my house to go to the game?" I asked Andy on our way home.

"Sneak out? I mean if a guy stole you straight from your room, then you could get out that way," Andy suggested.

"You're right. Thanks Andy! I should've thought of that!" I said looking down at my watch. "The game is in an hour. I've gotta get home and eat something." I ran ahead.

"Bye!" Andy yelled after me.

As I turned the corner, somebody touched my shoulder. After all that happened, I was so scared I jumped and halted to a stop.

"Girls. You guys are scared of everything," Coach Skylar said behind me.

"Oh. It's just you. The reason I'm scared is because some guy kidnapped me and I...yeah. You saw me on the news, didn't you?" I asked walking backwards.

"Um... No. Are you ready for the big game?" Coach Skylar asked.

"Yup. I just gotta eat something and sneak out," I said. "I'm grounded for staying too late at the park the other day."

"Oh. Interesting," he said sarcastically. He didn't sound like he cared about a word I said.

"Yeah. Well, I better get home," I said running. "See you at the game",

At HoMe...

"I'll take this bag of pretzels and go into my room and do my homework. See you when I'm done. I have a lot so I might not be done till say dinner? Good? Ok," I said grabbing some pretzels.

I ran to my room. I looked at my watch. A half hour left. I jumped onto my roof. I looked down and gulped. Long way down to jump. I forced my eyes open as I slid over the rain gutter, hung down and let go. I almost didn't make it. I stood up on my front lawn and looked around. I ran as fast as I can to the park and into the ball field. I was just in time. We were just about to start the first inning.

"You made it!" Coach Skylar said.

"Yes. Are we in the outfield?"

"Yup."

During the game I hit 2 home runs and scored 3 times. I got 3 outs on the other team and 1 of them was because I caught the ball on fly. My pitching was improving, too. My team won.

AfTeR tHe GaMe...

"You did awesome out there!" Skylar said.

"Thanks," I said smiling. I was finally earning his respect. "I gotta get home. Sorry."

"See you the next game. The sheet tells all," he said handing a light blue sheet to me. Our next game was the championship. After that we would *be* the champions, if we won (which I knew we would).

I ran home with the sheet in my hand.

At HoMe...

How was I supposed to get back into my room? I should've thought about that before I snuck out. I examined my house. I could stand on the fence and climb into my room, but that would require a lot of balance and if I got hurt I wouldn't be able to play. All of a sudden the most random thing popped into my head. Actually, the *two* most random things. The first one was, 'What am I going to be for Halloween', and the next one was, 'Do I like Coach Skylar?' I stopped and stared into space thinking. I shook my head and began searching for a way in. I ran to the back. I could use the back door and take the back steps. I slipped inside and walked up the steps.

I sat on my bed and pulled out a notebook from my backpack and began to do my homework. Right when I began my mom came in.

"Its time for dinner. Your homework will have to wait. How much do they give you in 4th grade anyway?" she asked laughing. I laughed too and put down the notebook. I really only had 1 thing for homework. I grabbed my mom's hand and we walked downstairs together.

SuNdAy...

I woke up at 9:00 AM and went downstairs to eat. I looked into the kitchen. My mom was looking at something. I think it was a picture. I looked down at the picture. Just at that moment I heard Little Sky cry. Mom stood up and stuffed the picture in her pocket. I turned and put my back to the wall. She walked the other way. I wondered who was in the photo that I didn't get to see. I ate and then went to Church, then my game. The championships.

ThE mIdDlE oF tHe GaMe...

We were loosing by 4 runs. I was up at bat. The bases were loaded and if I struck out, that would be 3 outs and the other team would be up.

The pitcher threw an underhand pitch. I got a strike.

"Pitch overhand!" I yelled.

He pitched overhand and I hit it. Not as far as last time, but far enough that the kids on second and third could run home. I was at 2nd base and Billy B was at third. We were now down by only two.

Next up was a kid named Jed. He made it to first, but nobody else could go anywhere. Then it was

Coach Skylar's turn. He hit the ball on the first pitch and sent Billy home. Everyone else moved up one. I was on 3rd, Coach Skylar was on 1st and Jed was in between. Next up was a short kid (named Freddy) who struck out.

We took the field. Freddy got one kid out, and Kevin, (a boy with red hair and lots of freckles) got another, and Coach Skylar got the last kid out. They did score 1 run before it was our turn at bat. We were down by 2 again.

Freddy, Coach Skylar, a kid named Sam, and I each scored in that inning. We won by 2! Everyone was so happy. We were all high fiving, dancing, cheering, and throwing our caps in the air. Out of the corner of my eye I saw George and Little Sky in his carriage stand up from the bench where they were resting and watching. George was smiling as he strolled away. While I was watching, Coach Skylar touched my shoulder. I spun around.

"The whole team is going out for lunch. Wanna come?" he asked.

"Sure," I said smiling.

"You did great! Without you, we wouldn't have won!" He said. Then he leaned down and whispered in my ear. "You're a pretty cool 9 year old."

I looked up. "How'd you know?" I laughed.

"I'm very smart! I knew since the beginning," he said. I shook my head and laughed lightly.

At HoMe...

When I got home, Mom was sitting on the couch next to Little Sky who was laying down holding something. I went over and looked into his little face. He smiled. He was holding a baseball and kind of sucking on it. He dropped it into my hand. I giggled. My mom gave me a kiss.

"George said that you did well in the game," mom said. "The one on Thursday, too."

I clenched my teeth. She knew!

"But I'm not punishing you because I know you like this sport. It's because you disobeyed me. Of course you're grounded, but you are still allowed to go to baseball. And, yes. You have to go to school," she said smiling. I giggled and smiled too.

LaTer tHat nighT...

Mom and George were downstairs talking and laughing. Little Sky was up here sleeping. I lay in bed thinking about the picture. I couldn't stand not knowing who was in it. I got up and walked down the hall to Mom's room. I was very nosy. I searched through her drawer till I found the photo. It was a picture of Lanette and me a while ago. I sniffled. I missed Lanette.

CHAPTER**NINE**

My 10th BiRtHdAy...

Everyone (my mom, George, Andy, and her family) cheered as I blew out the candles. This was a little party. I had had one with the whole family (George's family) the Tuesday before. I began to open my presents with Little Sky in my lap. He would turn 1 not so long after.

I opened the gift from Mom and George first. I opened the card. $100 dollars fell out. I smiled weakly trying to look excited as I read the card. I was excited, but I was never good at showing it. Then I opened the gift. It was a brand new baseball mitt and a wooden brown bat. I hugged my parents and opened the next gift. Two Bratz Dolls with really nice hair that I didn't like very much, but I knew I would probably wind up playing with them once or twice. I slapped on a fake smile at that one.

"Did you like all the gifts?" Mom asked picking up the wrapping paper.

"Yes," I smiled. "Andy and I are going to play dolls, OK?"

"That's fine, Hun."

Andy and I opened the dolls in my room.

"I don't like dolls," she said yanking on a piece of

48

plastic that wouldn't come off.

"Me neither, but they are fun to play with every once in a while." I sighed and tossed the empty box back behind my head. We were both silent for a moment trying to open the dolls without ripping their heads off. For a minute I remembered selling the dolls on the street.

"I think you like Coach Skylar," Andy said, still trying to yank one of the dolls' hairs out of the box. Why do they strap it in so tight anyway?

"No way," I said with a serious face. But deep inside I think I really *did* like him.

Andy got the doll out.

"Hey, Polly!" she said in a high-pitched voice, swinging the doll in my face. "You and Skylar look so cute together",

We laughed.

THe 3rd wEEk of SumMer...

"Wanna go for a swim in the lake?" Andy asked playing with a pebble on my front stoop.

"We can't. We have to watch Little Sky. Plus I have a game in, like, two hours," I said grabbing Little Sky as he tried to crawl away. I placed him in my lap and gave him a ball. He sucked on it and then threw it.

"Why can't you miss just one game?" Andy asked.

"Because then I won't know when the next game is," I said.

"If you have practice a week from today, which you do, ask Coach Skylar when the next game is," She said chucking the pebble. Little Sky cried. He wanted his ball. I sighed and reached down to get it, knowing he would just toss it again.

"What about Little Sky?" I asked.

"What about him? Your parents will be home in like 10 minutes!" Andy said. "Please come."

"Oh, fine. Stubborn brat. No offense," I said.

"None taken," Andy said.

At ThE laKe...

"I still don't feel right about skipping the game. The team needs me and I love baseball!" I said dipping my feet in.

"It's just one game," Andy said.

"Still. All the other games since the one when I snuck out were for fun. This game is the *championship* game!" I lied slipping my whole body in. We did have another championship coming up, I think. Baseball season never ended in the park, and we always had big games. Except if it snowed or rained. Then, we'd be delayed.

"Well, now that you're in the water you might as well stay," Andy said.

"Fine."

I reluctantly dunked under and swam around with Andy.

OnE wEeK lAtEr...

I began walking to the park for the practice. I felt bad about not going to the game. Someone tapped me on the shoulder. I knew who it was before I turned to look. Coach Skylar.

"Where were you during the last game? I was so worried-," He began. Then he cleared his throat. "I mean disappointed that you didn't come. We won, but it wasn't the same. I, I mean the *team* needs you",

"You were worried and you needed me?" I asked raising an eyebrow. We entered the park and walked

50

down the path to the ballpark.

"No I wasn't. I don't worry about girls. Especially 9 year old girls," He said playfully, but trying to say it like he meant it. Not in a mean way.

"Hey! First of all, I'm 10 now! Second, you were *too* worried! You even said it!" I bumped into him pushing him to the side. He did the same to me.

"Was not!" he said.

"Was too!" I laughed pushing him.

"Was not!" he bumped me.

"Was too!"

We continued that for a while until we stopped and looked at each other.

"Was too!" I said in a teasing voice. He leaned down and whispered: "Was too."

"Wait what?" I tried to say, but for some reason I couldn't. Was he agreeing this time? He leaned in and shut his eyes. This was going too fast for me. I started to fall back and time seemed to go in slow motion as I began falling. It isn't so clear to me what happened next, but I remember falling and my head hit something hard. I think my eyesight was blurry. I do remember seeing Coach Skylar lean down looking worried. "Polly! Are you all right?"

Then I blacked out.

WhEn I cOuld see Again...

I opened my eyes and blinked as everything slowly came back to me. There was a bright light shining in my eye. I slowly sat up and looked around. I was in... a hospital room? A doctor came into the room.

"Oh, young lady you're OK?" he asked with a faint accent. He was French, I think.

"Um...Yes," I said.

"Do you remember your name? Do you remember anything at all?" he asked coming closer.

"I'm Polly. Polly Brooks. I have a baby brother, Little Sky, a mom, a George, I mean step dad, and I play on a baseball team- "I began.

"Ok," the doctor said laughing. "I just wanted to make sure you could remember things. A young man carried you here about two hours ago. He told us your name was Polly and what had happened. He didn't know your last name so I couldn't contact your parents. The man is in the waiting room if you want to talk to him."

"Yes. That would be nice. Can I have something to drink?" I said.

"Sure thing," he responded and with that he left the room. A few minutes later, Coach Skylar was in the hospital room.

"Polly!" he said.

"Coach Skylar!" I said weakly. "What happened?"

He sat down. "Well, you were falling backwards, and your head hit a rock. Then I carried you here."

"Why would I fall?" I asked shaking my head.

"Um...Um..," he responded while grabbing at his collar. "Well, I was trying to...um... you kind of stumbled back like you were scared of something," he sighed.

"Ok. I'm hungry," I said quickly changing the subject. I knew exactly why I fell.

"Ok," he laughed, then remembered something, "OH! Almost forgot. I should call your parents! Do you remember your home number?" Coach Skylar pulled a cell phone out of his pocket.

"Um..." I thought for a moment. When I thought of one I told it to him. He tried it.

"Hello, I'm looking for Polly's mom," he said into

the phone. He put it down and held it to his stomach. "Do you know a little girl named Andy?"

"Yes. Ask Andy for the home number of POLLY BROOKS. Ok?" I said. Coach Skylar nodded and put the phone back up to his ear. He began to speak again telling Andy what I said. He rolled his eyes and put the phone down.

"She wants me to prove I'm not a guy trying to locate you and murder you," he said. I rolled my eyes and grabbed the phone.

"Andy! It's me! Polly! That was Coach Skylar!" I yelled into the receiver.

"Oh," Andy said.

"I, my head hit a rock and I don't remember my home number. I need to call my parents and tell them to come to the hospital," I said. Andy began saying things like "Are you OK?" and "Can I help in any way?" I told her to shut up and call my parents. She agreed and called.

"Hello?" Mom asked picking up the house phone.

"Hi, Mrs. Brooks," Andy said.

"Andy do you know were Polly is? She should be back from practice now," Mom said leaning against the kitchen wall.

"Yes, Mrs. Brooks. But before I tell you, what is your new last name because I keep calling you Mrs. Brooks."

My mom sighed. "Rachaka," she said.

"Ok. Polly is in the hospital. She got hit in the head with a rock," Andy said.

"Oh my gosh!" Mom said. "What happened? Where is she?"

"At the hospital," Andy said.

"I got that, but which one?" Mom said. I giggled to myself as I listened to this call (it was a three way).

"Ask her," Andy said. Skylar took the phone from me and gave my mother all the information.

"Oh, Polly!" my mom said as she burst into the hospital room. I was already deep in conversation with Coach Skylar. I looked up and smiled.

"You have bandages on your head and everything!" mom sat down on the bed and touched my face not noticing Coach Skylar.

"How did you get here? What happened?" Mom asked. I reached out my arms and grabbed Little Sky. I held him tight. He looked up at me and smiled. I laughed.

"Coach Skylar carried me. I..., my head hit a rock because I was falling because...," I stopped. "Because I was falling."

"Oh, hi Skylar! It's a pleasure to meet you," my mom said finally noticing him.

He just smiled and nodded his head.

"I feel fine, Mom. Honestly, I do. Where's George?" I asked mainly to show that I remembered him.

"Oh, he had to go pick something up at the store. Are you sure you're OK?" Mom asked.

"I'm fine, Mom. Really." I lightly placed the back of my hand to my head and tried to look faint. My mom didn't get the joke. She told me to stop it. At that exact moment the doctor came in with food and water.

"Well, Hello. You must be Polly's mother." The doctor put down the food and shook my mom's hand. The food didn't look very tasty.

"Now, what's wrong with my daughter?" she asked.

"Nothing. If she remembers everything. We gave her stitches on her head. Has there ever been another wound on her head because it seems like the rock opened a cut on her head," the doctor said. I hadn't known I got stitches. I guess I just kept sleeping or being knocked out, or whatever.

"Um, yes. She hit her head on the cabinet door the other day, but it was only minor."

"Well, she can be let out in a day or two. Here's what you must do to treat it."

I decided to take a nap at this point. When I woke up my mom wasn't there and neither was the doctor. Coach Skylar was still there.

"You're still here?" I asked.

"Your mom went home to sleep and the doctor left the room an hour ago," he said.

"Aw! You care about your team member so much! Even though she's a TEN year old girl," I said tilting my head to the side and smiling.

"I'm not going to fight with you over that. The most I can do is agree," Coach Skylar said. "I've gotta go. And by the way, you can just call me Skylar or just plain ol' Sky."

"Ok. Bye Sky," I said. Sky leaned down and kissed me on the cheek. I thought I was going to think, *Ew!* Or *Disgusting!* And then try to be polite by smiling, but I didn't think it was gross. I just smiled. I kind of liked it. Although, I didn't think he liked me liked me. It was just a generous kiss for a 10 year old with an injury, right?

CHAPTER**TEN**

A few WeeKs laTer on the DaY of our neXt game...

"**M**om, I have to go! It's baseball!" I said as I got up from the kitchen table.

"No. Not for another few weeks. When I feel your head is good enough to get you back into the game," Mom said picking up my bowl. I rolled my eyes.

"Mom it's been a few weeks. I'm fine."

George lowered his newspaper. "Let her go, Sweetie. Her head is fine."

"See George agrees."

"No," Mom said.

"It's fine George. I'll find a way to get to the game whether it be to sneak out or butter up Mom," I said standing up from the table. I kissed his cheek.

"Thanks for trying anyway." I went to take care of Little Sky who was crying.

"It's OK Little Sky." I cradled him in my arms. "If I can't go to the game I'll be at Andy's house",

I put Little Sky down. He was smiling. Then he started to cry again. I left him for Mom or George to take care of. Then I went to Andy's house.

At AnDy'S hOuSe...

"I'm glad you decided to miss another game to hang with me," Andy said. "You're getting too obsessed with that boyish sport."

"Andy. I came so you could cover for me while I'm at the game. I don't like to my baseball games," I said throwing my hands in the air. Andy frowned.

"Well first," she began linking her arm through mine. "Give me all the details on your big rock hit," I rolled my eyes and explained the whole story up to when I woke up.

"One question. Why did you fall?"

"Um...because there was a tree branch on the ground and I tripped."

"Then you would have fallen forwards. You said you fell backwards."

"Ok. Well Skylar was-"

"I thought you called him Coach Skylar."

"No. Skylar. Anyway. He was trying to..to...um... kiss me and I-"

"I told you!" Andy began to spin around and sing love songs.

"Will you let me finish?" I asked staring.

"Oh, yes. Go on," Andy said.

"I fell backwards because he was getting to close to my face and he never got the chance to kiss me, anyway."

"Well, he *was* at the hospital wasn't he?"

"Yeah. So?"

"Didn't he kiss you there?"

"Yes, but-"

"Oh snap! I'm right",

"Will you stop cutting me off? You know what? I've got a game to attend to. Cover for me, OK? See ya!" I said as I walked out the door. The phone began to ring. The usual phone call my mom makes to make sure I arrived safely.

At ThE pArK...

"Hey!" Skylar said waving at me.

"Hi," I said.

"You had to sneak out again?" Skylar asked. I nodded my head.

"Um. Why did you kiss me Skylar?"

"Because I owed you one. I missed the last time. Besides it was only on the cheek."

"Why did you try to kiss me that time?"

"Um...," Skylar blushed and I nodded.

"That's what I thought. You like me," I said putting on my mitt. I knew he didn't want to tell me he liked me.

"Wait that's-," he tried to protest, but we got called for the game.

I played pitcher the first inning. The second inning I got three strikes. I don't know what was wrong, but I couldn't concentrate. I shook my head. Every time I was up I struck out. My team lost that game.

"What is with you today?" a kid named Eric asked.

"I don't know," I said honestly.

I began to walk home.

"Hey! Polly! Wait up!" Skylar said.

"Don't ask me what was wrong because honestly I don't know," I said.

"Not that. I just wanted to walk home with you."

"I'm not going home. I'm going to Andy's house. And THEN home."

"Ok. Then I'll walk with you to her house."

This was scaring me. Skylar wanting to walk home with me. The kiss. What was with this? If he liked me, I wasn't ready. I was only 10! What was I supposed to do? I couldn't date.

"I can walk home by myself," I said as politely as possible.

"But I want to walk with you."

"I don't like to be protected and treated like a baby. I've gone through a lot and I could go through a lot more." I used this as an excuse instead of saying "Hey I like you, but I'm too young to date. Just treat me like a friend."

"That's not why I wanna walk with you! Wait up!" Skylar yelled chasing me. I wasn't really running. He was just far behind.

"Do you have a crush on me or something because I'm just 10. I'm only in 5th grade. Plus you're way older. You're in, like, 7th."

"Ok," he said stopping. "Maybe I like you, but that doesn't mean I was going to ask you out. I know you're too young for that. I just like to hang out with you. But if that's how you feel then-"

"It's OK." I stopped and shut my eyes. *Breathe in and out. Take deep breaths. Relax. Get rid of you temper.* "I'm sorry. You can walk with me."

Skylar was cute. I was surprised he didn't have a girlfriend. Maybe he did. How would I know?

At AnDy's houSe...

"Oh, and yes! How could I forget?" Skylar said as we laughed and talked together. "Some friends and I are going for pizza tomorrow in NEW YORK CITY",

"Wow!" I said. "Can I-"

"Do you wanna come?"

"Sure!" I said. "If my mom lets me. I gotta go."

"Ok. Bye!" Skylar said. I put my hand in front of my face and laughed.

"No kisses this time!" I laughed trying to make it a

joke, which it would have been before Skylar admitted he liked me. Skylar laughed too, but I could tell it was fake. A fake laugh to make a me happy.

"Polly",

"Yeah?" I asked turning.

"You have to get ready! Your mom called and said she was on her way to pick you up!" Andy said.

"I'm ready," I said. Andy cocked her head towards Skylar.

"The guy has gotta go," she said.

"Skylar. You have to-"

"It's OK. I know," Skylar said walking away.

LatEr at hOmE...

"Mom?" I asked at dinner.

"Can I go for pizza with Skylar and some friends in New York City?"

"No," Mom and George both said.

"Hey, Mom," I said

"NO," she said.

"I haven't met these people," Mom began. "And you shouldn't go without parental guidance. Besides, why do you have to go all the way to New York City to get pizza?"

"Mom," I said. "Mom, Mom, Mom. Of course there will be parental guidance. How do you think we'd get there otherwise?" I was lying. We were taking a bus to an area where we'd take the train to the city. I know this because I had called Skylar and asked. His number was on every sheet he gave the baseball team. I stuffed some mac and cheese into my mouth.

NeW YOrk CitY dAY...

"Hey, Polly!" Skylar said as I approached the park were I was supposed to meet him. There were three boys and one girl with him.

"Hi!" I said.

"This is Jake, Justin, Travis, and Jake's girlfriend, Melanie," Skylar said. He pointed to each person as he said their name.

"Hi!" they all said.

"Hi," I said in a pretty bored way.

At ThE pizZa PlAcE iN tHe CiTy...

"Table for..," Skylar began. He looked up into space and spent a second counting. "Six please. Table for six."

"Right this way." A guy who worked there showed us to a table.

We all looked at the menus and ordered our drinks. Then three girls walked in and smiled. They walked over to our table.

"Hi guys! What a coincidence meeting you here!" they said.

"Hi!" Melanie said. Melanie had silky brown hair. It waved a little. She was pretty. Melanie introduced the girls as Tina, Maria, and Jessica. Jessica had straight, long, shining black hair. Maria had short dark red hair. Tina had blonde hair that went a little past her shoulders. They were all pretty.

"May we join you?" the girls asked.

"Sure," everyone said. Besides me. I didn't like so many people. Part of me just wanted to be alone with Skylar. The other part wanted to have people there; just not so many people I don't know.

"You're late," Melanie whispered to them as the three girls pulled up chairs.

Maria pulled up a chair in between Melanie and me and started to talk to Melanie about clothes and makeup. Jessica pulled up a chair in between Jake and Justin. She went straight to talking with Justin. Melanie whispered something as Tina pulled up a chair. Maria moved next to Travis. She talked to him. Tina placed her chair right in between Skylar and me. She was talking to Skylar. I leaned back. I had no one to talk to now. This evening wasn't worth lying for.

"I love you in that shirt," Tina said to Skylar.

"And I like the way you look in that outfit," Skylar said. I sat up and felt a flare of jealousy.

"You should wear that shirt with a jacket or something during the back to school dance," Tina said fixing Skylar's collar.

"Oh, yeah!" Melanie said escaping from her deep conversation with Jake. "Who is everyone taking?"

"You," Jake said.

Everyone else didn't know.

Jessica was the first to comment on the 'I don't know'.

"Hey, Justin?" she asked.

"Yeah?" Justin said.

"Will you take me to the dance?" It sounded so casual. I liked listening to other people's conversations. Well, I didn't like all these people who I didn't know being there, but I liked to listen. Plus, to them I was invisible so nobody noticed. Nobody cared.

"Sure. Why not?" Justin said smiling.

"Hey, Maria. If you don't have a date I guess I could take you," Travis said to Maria.

"Sure," Maria said.

"Now we can all go together. Right, Tina?" Melanie asked turning to her friend.

"I've gotta go to the bathroom. Be back in a sec," I said slipping away. Nobody paid any attention. I didn't go to the bathroom. I just left the table. But I still listened.

"Not me and Skylar," Tina said.

"Why don't you guys go together?" Maria asked. I could tell that the girls had planned this whole thing. I tried to think what I usually thought with things like this; this is so stupid and lame. People that age aren't supposed to act like that. But for some reason, I couldn't help myself.

I didn't hear Skylar's response, but I could tell by the expression on Tina's face that Skylar said, "Yes."

"Ok. I'm back," I said slipping into my seat. Since their plan was over, they finally noticed me.

"Oh. Hi...um..," Melanie said. Before I could tell her my name, Skylar cut in.

"Polly. Her name's Polly," he said.

"Oh yeah. Why is she here again? Isn't she your little sister or something?" Melanie asked. Skylar opened his mouth to speak, but this time I cut in.

"I'm really not sure why I'm here. I think I'll be leaving now," I said pushing back my chair. I left the pizzeria without another word.

Surprisingly, I made it safely home. With my usual luck, I should have died before I made it back to New Jersey.

At HoMe...

"Hi, Mom," I said.

"Hi. You're home earlier than I thought. How was it?" Mom asked.

"It was OK. Not worth begging for. Can I go to Andy's house?" I asked to quickly change the subject.

"Sure, Hun," she said. So there I was on my way to Andy's house where I would have a friend named Andy who would make me unfold my whole love life story. I wasn't even supposed to HAVE a love life yet.

Better yet be so deep into it.

AnDy'S hOuSe...

"I heard you had a date with your boyfriend today," Andy said smiling as she ran her finger along her living room floor.

"It was not a date and he is not my boyfriend," I said.

"But you kissed him," Andy said.

"Huh. Like that means anything," I responded.

"Just tell me how it was."

"There was me, Skylar, three of his friends and one of his friend's girlfriend out for pizza. Then three girls came in and sat with us. Let's just say by the time that I left each girl and each guy at the table had a date for the Back to School Dance except me. A really pretty girl named Tina is going with Skylar. Nobody noticed me the whole time. Near the time when I left and people noticed me, this one girl, Melanie was her name, was like 'What's her name again? Why is she here? Isn't she your sister or something?' Then I got up and left," I explained.

Andy shook her head.

"Pops," she said.

"Pops are pretty popular girls who are total guy magnets. My brother and his friends are always talking about how hot pops are. Or they did. Now, they're all, like, getting married. Including my brother, as you probably know. You're invited to the wedding, but you have a baseball game that day," Andy said.

"I'll skip it for the wedding," I said.

Andy looked up. "Really?" she asked.

"Yeah," I said. "You know, Andy, I kind of, kind of...of...like LIKE Skylar. Kinda...a little."

"This is bad. I bet you Skylar is going to start to miss

every single baseball game to go make out with Tina now," Andy said wide eyes. We both stuck our fingers down our throat.

WaLkInG bAcK tO mY hOuSe...

"Polly!" someone called. I turned to see Skylar and his friends (including Tina, Maria, and Jessica) coming my way. I rolled my eyes.

"Why did you leave? That was really rude. Plus we left early to come get you and now I didn't get to eat!" Tina said rudely. From how thin she was I would have never once thought for a minute that she even ate anything.

"Yeah, what happened?" Jake asked.

"I left because...because... Look. I'm not Skylar's sister. I was there because Skylar, I mean, Coach Skylar asked me to come. He is my baseball coach. I'm the only girl on the whole damn team and I quit. I'm not that great anyway. And just for your information Tina you were the rude ones, OK? To you guys I was totally invisible!" I said. I walked away.

"Wait, Polly! You can't qui-," Skylar began, but Tina held him back.

"Don't run after her. It's pointless. She's just a stupid kid. Come to my house and we can relax in my hot tub," Tina said glaring at me and smiling deviously. I hate when people do that. It looks so creepy.

Skylar followed Tina only looking back once to see if I was there.

At HoMe...

I sat on the couch with Little Sky in my arms and picked up a blue sheet Skylar had given us recently. It showed the final games of the summer. There were three left. I decided I'd go to the games and watch.

If I couldn't play then I'd watch. I thought back to what I said and I wondered why I quit. I knew I shouldn't have. I put the blue sheet on the glass table in front of me. It was getting close to dinnertime. I placed Little Sky in his small kind of fenced off crawling area. He crawled around and played with his ball.

Saturday At ThE pArK...

I walked down the path and pushed my brother with me. I was going to watch one of the final games of the summer.

I sat on a bench to watch the game. It was an OK game. Our team had played better before, but we still won.

I cheered although in my head I was thinking about how they won with no help from me.

I heard a really loud cheer and looked around Tina stood up and ran down the bleachers headed towards Skylar. I thought about Tina. If I ever talked to her again she would be just as mean if not meaner than Icky Nicky. I stood up and walked over to Skylar making sure to keep an eye on the baby. I tapped his shoulder. He turned and smiled happy to see me. He opened his mouth to talk, but was once again interrupted.

"I'm sorry. I'm back on the team if that's OK with you Skylar," I said. Tina was coming. Just to make her mad and because I was starting to like *like* Skylar, I acted like I was flirting with him. Tina looked really mad. Ha! Who was the stupid one now?

"Try someone your age," he said. I suddenly became completely confused. Why was he being so mean? Tina smiled. She seemed happy.

"Oh, how cute is she?" Tina said walking to Skylar's side and putting her arm through his. "Well, we can't bother with her right now. We have a date. Oh and Congrats on winning Sky."

"Thanks!" he said. Then he kissed her. What was with that? What happened to the old Skylar? Did Tina change him? Or was that me?

On ThE wAy HoMe...

"You there!" someone said. I didn't even turn around. I knew it was Skylar.

"What do you want?" I asked.

"I see how much you looked up to me as a baseball player so I have an autograph for you," Skylar said. I knew he was kidding, but I still rolled my eyes and stopped.

"No, Skylar. I don't want your autograph. I don't want to have anything to do with you. You changed. I don't care about you anymore," I said. Then I began to walk again. I actually started to cry a little. Skylar ran up in front of me. I stopped.

"It was a joke," Skylar said jumping in front of me.

"Please move. I need to get home," I said. When I looked up Skylar looked just as hurt as I was.

"I'm sorry. I truly am. When you said that thing to my friends and me the other day I felt bad. So I changed into something people would like better. I didn't expect it to affect you. I didn't expect you to care at all. I thought you didn't like me that way," Skylar said.

"I do. I just think that this stuff is too overrated for me. I also felt jealous when you agreed to go out with Tina. Where is Tina anyway?" I explained.

"Tina had to go study. I'll walk you home. We can start from here and work our way up," Skylar said grabbing my hand, as I pushed my brother's carriage with the other.

We walked home talking and laughing like nothing was wrong. I trusted Skylar. As a friend.

A bloCk Away FroM Home...
"Polly?" Skylar asked.
"Yeah?" I responded.
"If I don't go to that thing with Tina, she'll make up rumors about me and I'll loose all my friends. Is it OK if I just go with her so I won't loose my friends?" Skylar asked.
"OK." I didn't skip a beat. I just smiled.
"Thanks, Polly! You're the best."
"About the way you acted before."
"Yes. I know. I acted like a looser."
"You're coming to the next two games, right?" Skylar asked. "To actually *play*?"
"Yes. I am," I said.
"I thought babies were supposed to cry," Skylar said gesturing to Little Sky.
"Not him. He just sleeps. His name is Skylar just like your name, but I call him Little Sky. He's my brother." I looked down at him. Little Sky was sleeping as per usual.
"I'm going to go inside now," I said.
"OK," Skylar said. This time he didn't try kissing me. I was very happy.

1st dAy of 5th graDe...
"Polly? Have you noticed how Icky Nicky stinks at being mean?" Andy asked on our way to school.
"Yup," I said. I was kicking a rock and trying to see if I could kick it all the way to school.
"Why are people intimidated by her?" Andy asked. I shrugged my shoulders.
"I dunno," I said.

We arrived at school and ran in. We were excited to see our new teachers.

Andy and I were in different classes again. I was stuck in Icky Nicky's class again.

Icky Nicky was showing off the new cell phone and I-pod her parents had gotten her for her birthday.

"And, just to celebrate, I baked cupcakes for the whole class. Even the dorks," Icky Nicky said turning to me. Then something randomly popped into my mind. I remembered Tina. The one who was *going* to be my friend? What had happened to her? I wasn't sure.

"So you *did* bake one for yourself," I said smiling. Some kids, including Dana, laughed.

"Anyway, here. Everybody take one," Icky Nicky said opening a box to reveal cupcakes. We all grabbed one. There were 5 left over.Upon finishing my first, I picked up another.

"Hey," Icky Nicky said. "You can't have two. I said to take *one*."

"Well, Icky Nicky, you should always have more than one. You never know if it might be your last. Especially with your cooking," I said taking a bite of the cupcake. Icky Nicky tried to throw a cupcake at me, but it hit the blackboard right where it said "Ms. Rinnig."

"Oh no you didn't!" I said. I smashed a cupcake onto her clothes.

"This is my new mini skirt outfit!" Icky Nicky barked. I laughed.

"And I care... why?" I asked shaking my head.

Just then, Ms. Rinnig walked into the room.

"What is going on in here?" she yelled. Icky Nicky started to cry. Don't feel bad for her. She was faking it.

"Polly went crazy. She threw a cupcake at me,

threw a cupcake at the board, and tried to hurt me. I did nothing. I was just trying to make everyone happy by sharing my cupcakes," Icky Nicky cried. I rolled my eyes.

"Go to the principal's office, Polly",

"Wait!" a little voice said. It was Tina. The girl who narrowly missed becoming my friend.

"Nicky called Polly a dork then Polly told a joke. Then Polly went to get another cupcake and Nicky said no, but Polly already started eating it. Then Polly made another joke and Nicky tried to throw a cupcake at her, but it missed. It hit the board. Then Polly put cupcake on Nicky's dress. Then Nicky started to pretend cry so you would believe her," Tina said.

"Is this true, class?" the teacher asked. I thought it had sounded weird the way Tina used the word joke. The whole class said yes and Icky Nicky had a little lunch with the principal. HA!

"Hey, Polly! Wait up!" Tina yelled as I ran outside. Recess was the one time of day I could play with Andy so I was anxious, but I waited. "Can I play with you at recess today?"

"OK. But I usually play with Andy, is it OK if she plays too?" I asked.

"Fine with me," Tina said laughing.

AfteR sChOol...

"I had fun with Tina," I said walking backwards.

"She's an OK girl. She is the kind of girl who would turn on you out of fear so I wouldn't trust her with secrets that Icky Nicky can use against you," Andy said. I nodded my head. Then I saw Skylar up ahead.

"Yo, Skylar!" I yelled. He turned around and would have usually smiled when he saw me, but he didn't this time.

"Hi. Listen, Polly, we need to talk," he said. I turned to Andy who was still staring at Skylar. I ran ahead to talk to him.

"Polly, I'm moving. To the town that all my friends live, where my school is, were my dad's job is, and um... Tina. The thing is, I really like you, but I'm going to be kinda far. Tina is there and she likes me. She's just closer. And I like her enough so...yeah," Skylar said.

"OK," I said quietly looking up at him.

"Oh, but I have two surprises for you. Surprise number 1," he began, "You get to be the new captain of our baseball team. But before you get excited, I got you something to remember me with," Skylar pulled something out of his pocket. It was a silver ring that had 'Polly and Skylar' on it in script. It was beautiful. I gave him a hug and walked away before he could say anymore. It would get too dramatic. Andy caught up to me as I was slipping the ring on my finger. I rarely put rings on my ring finger. Always on my middle or pointer, but not this time.

"He's moving. Tina will be closer to him when he moves," I said. I kind of wanted to cry, but I didn't. I knew I'd have other boyfriends, but I also knew I would never have another first boyfriend. Even if I didn't want him to be, I guess in a way you could have called him my boyfriend.

At HoMe...

I slid into my chair and held my hands out for prayer before dinner. Tonight it would just be George, Little Sky and me. Mom was out with my Aunt Melinda and some friends of hers. Little Sky clearly did not like the food he was given. He spit it all out onto his high chair and then he stuck his face in it. Now he was one year old and starting to become like most boys. Sicko.

"How was your day, Polly?" George asked as he cleaned up Little Sky's mess.

"Fine." I looked down at the ring, "Just fine. How was your day?"

"All right I guess," he said.

I picked at my food. Without Mom, George and I couldn't start a dinner worthy conversation.

"I think I'm done. I'm not so hungry," I said. I stood up and went to my room.

School...

"Andy?" I shifted my backpack around on my shoulders.

"Yea?" she asked. She was dragging a stick along the ground.

"Ya know how sometimes people keep secrets from people just to 'protect them'?"

"Yup."

"In the end, it always turns out they should've told the secret and that would've made things better. Don't you think some people, like me, have been through enough that those secrets would inflict no pain on them if they were told?"

"Um...yes...ok that was random, but yes."

We walked inside and Andy threw the stick aside.

"See you at recess," Andy said, going over to join some of her friends.

ThAt NiGhT...

George got sick with a cold. It wasn't bad at all, but Mom would not let him touch the baby. I told her that the baby was older now so he had a stronger immune system. I was kind of smart for my age, but I wasn't exactly sure if I was right.

"I don't need George to help me right now. He's sick and I'm not taking chances even if it *is* just a cold," Mom said. She collapsed on the couch and yanked a pillow under her head. Little Sky kind of walked and hobbled half way towards my mom then fell. He gave up and just crawled to her. Then he decided to poke her and he laughed. She smiled and ruffled his hair. Then she shut her eyes. That left me to care for the baby.

"Let's go watch TV, Little Sky. I think "Degrassi," is on and Andy says it's a good show." I picked him up. He laughed at pretty much everything nowadays.

I turned on the TV. I caught the last two minutes of "Degrassi," then turned off the TV and sighed. I didn't get that show. There was a copy of The Omen on the table. George had rented it. I picked up the DVD and laughed. Devil Child. The Devil wouldn't send anyone to Earth. I knew that. *Wait!* I thought *the Devil sent me to Earth.*

I had completely forgotten about the Devil thing. I put down the DVD. I wondered how I had gotten to hell in the first place and how I survived all the pain...no love...I had no idea what my mission was either. I didn't think the Devil sent me either. I tapped my chin.

"Polly?" a stuffed up nose said.

"Yes?" I jumped.

"I didn't know you let your brother play with your hair."

Sure enough, Little Sky was standing on a pillow, holding my shoulder, and a few strands of my hair.

"I don't." I picked Little Sky up off the pillow and placed him on the floor. Mom was sleeping.

"Polly!" Little Sky said.

"He said my name! George! Mom! He said-," I

73

looked around. George had left. I woke my mom up.

"You missed it! Little Sky talked!"

"Really?" Mom stood up, "Say Mommy! Say Mommy",

"Polly!" He giggled.

I made a look like I was so special. "He can say MY name",

"Polly!" Little Sky stretched out his arms. I picked him up again. Mom kissed both of us.

"He can't say anything more important, but ..,"

"Mom!" I injected.

CHAPTER**ELEVEN**

OnE wEek lAteR...

"**S**o he can say 'Polly' now?" Andy asked looking into Little Sky's crib. Her hair fell in his crib and he didn't like that. He started blinking like crazy.

"Polly!" Little Sky said as he yanked on Andy's hair.

"I guess that's a yes." She flipped her hair over her shoulder and pulled it back into a ponytail.

"Polly! Andy",

"Hey, Polly, he could say my name to",

"No Andy. That was George." I turned around to face George. I stood in a soldier like position. Then Andy copied me.

"Yes, Sir?" We said.

"I'm taking your mother, well not Andy's...," George began.

"I get it George. Mrs. George not my mom," Andy said.

"Ok then. So I'm taking her for her mammography."

"Mommy has breast cancer?" I freaked out.

"No. Every woman over some age has to take the test like once a year. I'm just dropping her off, but I'm also going to get some food for us. The appointment is two towns away. It might take a while. DO NOT OPEN THE DOOR FOR ANYONE EXCEPT ANDY'S PARENTS OR ME. Check the caller ID before answering the phone and only answer if its-"

"You or my parents," Andy cut in. I was a lot less nervous now.

"And we can't leave the house. We know," I added.

"Got it. Bye, George!" We said together.

"Bye, girls." George picked up Little Sky and went into the car with my mom.

"Now what should we do?" Andy asked lying on the couch.

"It's Saturday." I jumped over the back of the couch and sat next to her.

"So?" Andy asked.

"I don't know. I was just saying." I started to play with her hair.

"I feel like eating popcorn. Wanna watch a movie and eat popcorn?"

"Ok," I said, "I'll make the popcorn you pick the movie."

I stuck the popcorn in the microwave.

"I would make Jiffy Pop, but I don't think we should use the stove," I told Andy.

"How bout *Grease*?" Andy asked pulling out the videotape.

"Ok."

We sat on the couch watching *Grease* and eating popcorn. When we reached the part where Rizzo and the other girls (I forget their names) were wearing wigs while making fun of Sandy, the doorbell rang.

I peaked through the window. My eyes grew wide.

"Fungu I'm Sandra Dee!" Andy sang along with the TV.

"Andy!" I whispered, "My dad is outside."

"Should we open it?" Andy asked. Sometimes Andy could just be so dumb.

"Of course not! He is supposed to be in prison. And you heard what George said: 'Only open the door for me or Andy's parents.'" I gave her a look that showed the answer was totally obvious.

"And I bet he isn't here just to say 'Hello!' to you," Andy agreed.

I gulped remembering that he went to prison for murder, and I was the one who ratted him out. "Let's lock ourselves in the back bathroom."

"Ok," Andy said grabbing the phone and the paper with George's number on it.

In the bathroom we called George.

"Hello?" George said.

"George? It's Polly."

"And Andy," Andy added.

"What's up?" George asked.

"My dad is here. At the front door. MY DAD."

"I'll be right home. Go hide in one of the bathrooms or under the beds," George said, "Love you, Bye",

I could tell how nervous George was.

Andy and I looked at each other hopefully.

"I hope his car goes fast," Andy said.

"Is he still there?"

Andy peeked through the door. "Yes."

"Uh-oh," I gulped.

"Polly?"

"Yes, Andy?"

"Now your dad is watching TV in your living room?"

Andy and I hugged each other tightly wondering why he was here, how he got in, and what if he had to go to the bathroom. The last thought left me after remembering the fact that my dad didn't know where the bathroom was.

"I have never in my whole life been so afraid of my dad."

"Me neither. Well not your dad, my dad." Andy laughed and then cupped her hands over her mouth. I began dialing for George.

"What?" Andy asked.

"I'm asking George if we can-"

Knock Knock

"Hello? Is anybody in there?" Dad asked from outside the door. Andy jumped up and unlocked the latch on the window. She opened it all the way and tried to get out. She escaped on the second try. We heard more knocks and I quickly jumped out the window.

"Polly? Are you still there?" George's voice said. I put the phone to my ear.

"Sorry, George. Listen, Andy and I will be right outside waiting for you. We had to climb out the window. We got too scared. He was coming into the bathroom so we had to-"

"Escape," a voice above us said. My dad was looking down at us through the window.

"Polly? Polly? Are you all right?" George's voice came out of the receiver. I dropped the phone to the ground.

"Hi Dad," I said.

"Now why would you be afraid of me? I just came to say hello."

We then heard a car pull up in the driveway. We ran to the driveway, but it wasn't George's car. Two big men came out. Andy and I screamed, but the big men cupped their hands over our mouths and held us back from running. By this point Andy and I were crying. I heard my dad run through the house making his way into the driveway. Just then George's car pulled up. George jumped out of the car and punched the two big guys in the head. He did it so fast the big guys didn't see it coming. I named the big guys Buckweed and Shirly after two guys I saw in a movie who looked like them.

"I'm back, but I don't have any food yet," George said.

George walked into the house and we followed close behind.

"George, where's Little Sky?"

"At the test with your mom. I wouldn't dare take him with me."

My dad appeared from behind the inside of the door.

"Mr. Brooks leave my home or I will be forced to call the police," George said. I knew George would call the police even if my dad did leave.

"I just came to see how my wife and daughter were doing. No harm done," my father said. I had a very, *very* strong feeling that he was lying. My dad punched George in the face and they got into a fight. Andy and I were screaming and crying. George got knocked out and my dad turned towards Andy and me. We ran. We didn't stop running. We were about half way to town and still running.

"Andy!" I cried, "I'm getting tired."

"Me too," Andy said between breaths.

"Why do bad things," I took a breath, "always happen to me?"

Then I collapsed on someone's lawn. Water from

the sprinkler flew across my flushed face as everything became darker.

"Not again," I whispered as I saw Andy land next to me, "not again."

SoMe PeRsOn'S hOuSe...

I blinked a few times and sat up. I was on a couch in someone's home.

"Hello?" I asked. "What-," I was cut off as I felt water being practically shoved into my mouth. I drank it.

"You fainted. Probably from dehydration or something like that. So did your friend," A lady said.

I looked up and raised my eyebrows.

"Aren't you, like, my old kindergarten teacher?" I asked.

"And you are?" she asked.

"Polly Brooks."

"What were you doing before you ended up here?"

"I was running from my father."

"Why were you doing that?"

I saw why I wasn't so fond of my kindergarten teacher. She wasn't so friendly. This made me think about the times when love was a weird feeling to me. By this time, as in the time that I fainted on this lady's lawn, I was used to it.

"He's a fugitive. Is Andy awake?"

"If you're talking about the girl with the long dark hair, then yes she's in the kitchen."

"I need to get back to my house. My step dad is unconscious on the kitchen floor and that's not good," I said about to stand up. I could tell I was scaring this lady with the whole fugitive thing and stuff. I was scared myself.

"I'm calling the police," She said, "Where do you live?"

I told her my street address and then she took Andy and me back to my house.

When we got there, my dad, Buckweed, and Shirley D. Were nowhere to be found. My mom was talking to the police and George was on the couch sleeping or knocked out I'm not sure which one.

"Honey where were you?" Mom said hugging my tightly.

"I fainted on that lady's lawn," I said.

"Polly, tell me everything," the police officer said.

I told the whole story with exact detail and Andy and the lady added in some parts. The police officer promised that he and other officers would try and find my father and then left.

Little Sky walked over and tugged on my pants.

"Polly!" he said. We both smiled. Little Sky gave me a hug and a kiss.

"I'm just glad you're Ok," Mom said.

"My brother is getting me an iPod Nano for my birthday," Andy said.

"That was random," I said laughing weakly.

LaTeR tHaT nIgHt...

"Mom?" I asked.

"Yes?" she replied scrubbing something off a dish.

"Why do bad things always happen to me?" I asked.

Mom stopped washing dishes for a moment.

"Polly, with every bad thing, there's a good thing and God has a plan for everyone. You have to re-member all of the good things in you life too. Things happen for a reason, they are supposed to happen that way. You'll have a good life in the end. Trust me," she said. *Maybe bad things happen because people don't want me to complete my mission.* I thought.

"But, Polly, there is something about you that is different from everyone else. Something special. I mean, everyone's different, but there is something about you. I know that in the end you'll be happy," Mom explained, "You have plenty of life left to live."

"Mom?"

"Yes?"

"Never mind." I looked down at my feet.

"No tell me. You can tell my anything." Mom said.

"You wouldn't believe me."

"Try me," Mom said. I bit my lip. I wanted to tell her about my Devil mission and all, but I wasn't sure if I should.

"Mom, before I was born, I was in hell with the Devil. He said he was sending me on a mission on earth. He let me plan my life for earth. I planned this life of riches and cute boys and nothing goes wrong and it's so much fun, but then I was born in a box. Mom it was a box. My life is exactly the opposite of what I planned." I explained this very slowly.

Mom just stared and chuckled. "Why would you make up such a weird story?"

"I told you that you wouldn't believe me! It's true, but no matter who I tell in the future, nobody I know will ever believe me. I know it for a fact. Who is going to believe Polly Brooks is Devil Girl? Who is going to believe that she was in hell with her skin burning off and living in pain? Who is going to believe that she planned her whole life, but it all went wrong? Nobody. For some reason I cried. This was a very strange thing. I had never told anybody about this before and I would think my mom would believe me, but of course, she didn't. Now, if I would tell *anyone*, I know for a fact you'd have to be one of the most gullible people on earth to believe it. *Which is why I don't ex-*

pect any of my readers to believe it even though it's true.

"NOBODY!" I yelled. I started to walk down the hall to the stairs when I felt a tug on my pants. I looked down. Little Sky was holding out his arms and calling my name.

"Not right now Little Sky," I said rubbing one eye. I ran into my room and Little Sky started to cry.

ThE nExT dAy...

"We're going to Church now, Polly," George said when I finished breakfast. Mom said she wasn't feeling good and stayed in bed. "We haven't been to Church in a while."

"Ok," I said.

After Church I went to Andy's house. We were debating and arguing.

"Stop thinking about Skylar, Polly!" Andy said, "Why won't you just get over him! No offense, but what you had wasn't so special. It was really kind of random. It's just a girl who likes her baseball coach and he likes her back. Not really anything big."

"I miss him and I don't think I'll get over him so easily. Besides, you were the one who said I liked him."

"You quit your favorite sport because he moved."

"You don't care that I quit baseball, Andy. I have to go. I have a haircut appointment in a half hour."

In ThE cAr...

George's phone rang. He picked it up and talked for a minute then hung up.

"I'm dropping you two off at Aunt Malinda's. The doctor called and he needs Mom for a second," George said.

"Since when do we go there?" I asked.

"Since now," George said.

AuNt MaLiNdA's HoUsE...
"I hope it's not too much Malinda," George said.
"Of course not! I love them so much!" she started kissing us like crazy. I went inside and sat on her couch watching TV.
"How old are you, Polly?"
"10," I said. I switched the channel to *Teen Nick*. *Ned's Declassified School Survival Guide* was on.
"You're in 5th grade? Wow!" Aunt Malinda said. "How old is Skylar?"
"He is 1 and a half."
"Do you like cookies?" she asked. I smiled and nodded.
"I think I'll make some."
"Ok," I smiled, "I'll be exploring."
"I went upstairs into the attic. The place looked like it hadn't been touched in 20 years. It was dark, dusty, and small. There were photo albums in one corner next to some games, and the rest of the attic was filled with boxes and containers. There was a tiny window in the back next to a tiny door. The attic creeped me out. I grabbed a photo album and went downstairs. I sat on the couch admiring the cover. It was very elaborate with green and gold sparkles and a lace border. I opened the cover. There was a picture of Aunt Malinda in a wedding dress in front of a Cathedral.
"Aunt Malinda?" I asked.
"Yes?" she poked her head into the room.
"What ever happened to your husband?"
"He never showed up at the wedding. I haven't seen him again since."
"Oh. I'm sorry," I said turning the page as Aunt

Malinda sat down next to me.

"It's ok. That's me, George, and our sister Tiffany who moved to Hawaii. I was 17, George was 20, and Tiffany was 26."

"That's George, me, and your mom," Aunt Malinda pointed to another picture.

"You knew my mom back then?"

"George and your mom have been friends since they were kids."

She pointed to another picture, "There is me and my cat Shadows."

"There is me, George, Jake, and your mom."

"There is me and some other guy."

She went on and on about the pictures until my mom called. It was time to go home. I was worried about my mom. Why did the doctor want to see her again?

In ThE cAr...

"Polly?" Mom asked.

"Yes?"

"Was that story you told me true? Be honest."

"What would you say if I said yes and what would you do if I said no?" I asked face against the window.

"Polly, I don't know."

"Yes. It was a true story, but I'm not evil like the Omen or anything. I wasn't planning on telling anybody. I still think you don't believe me. I guess my life isn't so horrible. I just wish I could figure out what went wrong and what my mission was. But I'm not so sure it was the Devil that sent me anymore."

"I think I know what your mission is, Polly, and I don't think the Devil sent you either. You will find out when the time comes. I love you."

"Don't tell anyone." I began playing with my ring.

Maybe someone believed me after all.

At HoMe...
Mom unlocked the door. "I need to tell you something important, Polly."
"What?" I asked.
"I'm not sure how to tell you this. Please don't get scared."
"Go on, Mom."
"I have breast cancer, Polly."
"What? Are you going to leave me?" My eyes filled with tears.
"Polly, everyone has to die, but I'm going to try and fight this cancer. I will give it my all."
"I don't know anybody who died," I said shaking my head.
"Yes you do Polly. Don't be stubborn."
"Lanette is still alive she's just somewhere else." I tried to sound mad, but I was overwhelmed by sadness.
"I'm sorry Polly."
"This isn't fair. I'm going to loose you like I lost Lanette",
"What's with all the fighting and crying?" George asked as he walked in from the back yard.
"Mom has cancer." I wiped my face with the back of my hand. Then I went and sat on the couch. Little Sky cried and ran over to me he put his face in my lap. George hugged mom and then whispered something in her ear. He kissed her and she walked over to me.
"Polly, I'm sorry. I didn't know how to tell you so I just went right out and said it. I can't help it if things like this happen. I can't help it if bad things happen to you. I *can* help you get through all your hard times.

Even if I'm not there," Mom explained. She looked like she was going to cry too.

I hugged my mom really, really, really tight. I hugged her like I'd never let go. I didn't want to. It felt like if I let go I'd never see her again. I told myself she wasn't going to die and that everything would be ok. I knew she would be treated, but deep inside I had doubts...

"It's getting late," George said.

"You should get to bed," Mom agreed.

"Ok," I said.

Little Sky held out his arms. I picked him up and kissed him.

At ScHoOl...

"How did your mom's test go?" Andy asked as I unpacked my books. Andy was done with everything so she had snuck into my classroom before the bell rang.

"I don't wanna talk about it." I continued unpacking my books.

Icky Nicky came and pushed all my books off my desk. They scattered around the floor.

"Oops! Sorry, Polly!" Icky Nicky laughed. I kicked her really hard in the shin.

"Listen Icky Nicky, I've had it with you. You're a mean stupid liar who picks on me for no reason besides that you just can't get over the fact that I was just born better than you and I'll always be better than you." I kept a smug look on my face to further prove the fact I was better.

"Well, well...," Icky Nicky struggled to stand up.

"You made a big mistake!" Icky Nicky smiled. My first fight was upon me. Icky Nicky knee kicked my stomach and slapped me as a tall kid named Jason moved all the desks to make an arena. A few kids were screaming fight. Andy stood in the doorway biting her nails. She had to leave, but was so eager to stay and watch.

"This'll be easy," I muttered to myself. Icky Nicky looked satisfied. I kicked the back of her leg causing her to fall down and then a kick to her stomach while she was off guard. I hit her and pushed her. She fell against the desk and cried as some kids ran over to help her. Nobody had noticed the teacher standing in the back of the room.

"Nicole and Polly go to the principle's office IMMEDIATELY!" she shouted. I groaned and made my way through the group of kids and into the hallway where Andy wished me luck before escaping to the refuge of her own classroom.

At least I won... I thought.

tHe PrInCiPaL's OfFiCe...

"What's wrong with you two?" Dr. Jimono yelled.

"Polly has been mean to me ever since Kindergarten for no reason!" Icky Nicky faked a cry.

"No Ick- I mean Nicky. That's what you did to me. And I know the principle will take your side because you're a good liar. My life is so unfair. Since I know the principle in going to end up blaming me, I'll be on my way." I sat up and walked towards the door of the small office.

"Polly you sit right back down here! We're not done yet!" Dr. J said.

"Dr. Jimono, I did it. I started the fight by teasing and kicking Polly. Punish me not her." Was that actually Icky Nicky? Yes! It was!

"Is this true?" Dr. J turned to me. I was too astonished to speak causing him to take my answer as a yes.

"Come to my office instead of your classroom

everyday from Tuesday to Thursday. That's three days suspension. I'll send in a note to your teacher to remind you," Dr. J explained to Icky Nicky, "And as for you," he turned back to me, "Stay out of trouble." I nodded.

When we were out of the principal's office, Icky Nicky just walked past me back to the classroom.

During recess, there was a crowd in the corner of the concrete yard. I walked over to the crowd to see what was up.

"She was too scared and selfish to say anything so I took the blame because I'm brave and I'm a nice person," Icky Nicky explained to the crowd. "Little Polly, she is just so mean to me. For no reason! Well that doesn't matter because I have all of you and she has nobody because *I'm* so much *better* than *her*."

My mouth dropped open. I had the strongest urge to go up there, call her an '#&**!^%!$# ' or something and beat the crap out of her. Of course I didn't do that. Everyone would just believe her even more. I thought, and thought, and thought. When I stopped thinking, I noticed people were staring at me and whispering. One girl passed me by and whispered, "How come you're so mean to her?"

I just walked over to the side and waited for Andy. *"Some people are so immature. Just drop it Polly. Who cares? None of those people were ever your friends anyway," I* said to myself.

I thought and waited. I sighed and waited some more. I looked at my watch. Recess was almost over. Then I saw Andy walking towards me.

"What's up?" Andy asked.

ThAt NiGhT...

I stayed in bed and shut my eyes trying to sleep. I

stayed there for what seemed to be forever before drifting off to sleep.

I opened my eyes. I yawned and blinked. I looked around noticing I was in a chair in a room with pinkish purple walls and magenta carpeting. There was a little brown table in front of me and three chairs.

"Polly." Skylar appeared in the chair across from me and called to me. I opened my mouth to talk, but I couldn't.

"Hello, Polly." Tina appeared in the chair next to me and blew Skylar a kiss.

"Did you ever wonder why that man kidnapped you, Polly?" Skylar reached under the table and pulled out a cup of coffee and sipped it.

"Yes. The answer goes far back into history." Tina flipped her hair and smiled. I didn't understand what was going on or what they were talking about. For some reason, of all the questions that filled my head, not one of them was 'Where am I?'

"History, Polly. Do you see the stimulation of history between time and space? What would it feel like if you were never born? Never became part of this earth?" Skylar leaned forward and his eyes opened wide. *What...what is that supposed to mean? The words don't make sense when they were put together like that. Not at all. Are they trying to tell me something? Simultaneous? Between time and space? Never born?* I thought. The words jumbled around in my head. I mixed the words around in the sentence trying to make some sense out of this.

"Well, Polly. I think you've heard enough. On to Analise." Tina yanked me into standing position and shoved me through a door I hadn't noticed before.

On the other side of the room it was pitch black. I couldn't see or hear anything. Out of fear I turned to the spot where the door was, but no door. Instead I saw the Devil standing there and laughing at me. Eyes glaring, fire surrounding him. I stumbled back and fell. Down, down, down, down. I landed unharmed in my room on my bed. I ran towards my door. It was locked and all of a sudden I grew small. I felt a hand touch my back. It was a girl my age. She looked beautiful in her white garments at first, but then scars appeared on her face, one even going right thought her eye. The white was stained red with blood. Her hair, some gone, some remaining.

"Polly," she said, "Don't fear this." I was now even more confused and scared than before. What was she talking about?

"I'm here for you, Polly. For you, to keep you safe," the girl said. I heard soft music. No more than the same few notes being played over and over again. The girl turned into a younger version of herself. Clean, healthy, no cuts or bruises. She wore regular kid clothes and sat playing the notes over and over again on the piano. A book sat in front of her. The pages flew until the book opened to a page that read Analise in big script letters.

"I'm starting to remember more of the song. I kind of remember how it goes," The girl, I guess named Analise, added a few notes to the song. "How it goes. How it goes. I remember it from one of my fears. A dream. A dream full of fears. A dream of fears that all came true."

She played faster and faster, as her face got madder, and madder. She kept adding more to the song until she just smashed the piano to bits with her bare hands. She turned to me and started shouting my name.

I blinked and sat up, breathing heavily. I thought

someone was beside me, but noticed it was just me I was hearing.

"Just a dream," I mumbled to myself. "Just a dream," I took deep breaths. I wondered if the dream had meant something, or was it just a nightmare. I went downstairs for breakfast, wiping a tear from my cheek.

Little Sky was hitting the table on his high chair with a spoon. Mom was getting all of us breakfast.

"Morning," Mom said.

"Morning, Mom," I said in a bored voice. I sat down at the table.

"Hi, Polly!" Little Sky laughed as if he had just seen the funniest thing in the world.

Mom placed a plate in front of me. I felt a kind of squeeze on my finger. I looked at my hand. Was the ring getting too tight already? I tried taking it off. It was too tight.

"Be right back." I smiled at my mom and escaped to the bathroom I used soap and water to take the ring off. Then I stared at it for a while. I thought about Skylar and the whole baseball team. I thought about what would've happened if Skylar hadn't left. I thought about my dream. When I thought about it, I could vaguely recall seeing Analise before the dream. But where? I sat on the stool under the sink and tried to remember. My mom suddenly opened the door.

"Polly?" she said. I jumped and hit my head hard on the sink.

"Ow," I said.

"Oh my gosh! Polly, are you all right?" Mom asked. I shook my head.

"I just hit my head. I'm fine," I said standing up.

We walked into the kitchen just as George came

down. He went outside to get the paper.

I ate quickly until George came inside with the paper and sat down. The cover showed the scariest thing I had ever seen. On the cover was a picture of Analise getting taken away by the ambulance? Her face covered in scars and clothes stained with blood. I dropped my fork and it made a clattering sound in my plate. Everyone turned towards me.

"What's wrong? You were just eating like a bottomless pit a second ago," Mom said.

"Who is that?" I asked staring at the cover of the paper.

"Um...," George read the caption. "Analise Brooks."

"Read me the story," I said. *That's my last name* I thought.

The story was about a little girl named Analise Brooks. They found her in a large house with staircases that led to nowhere and doors that led to walls. She was cut and bloody. There was nothing in the house but bits of what seemed to be a piano. There was nobody else in the house. People who lived nearby the house said they never saw anyone, but heard music being played from the house.

"Oh my gosh!" I started crying.

"What's wrong, Polly?" Mom said running to my side.

"I...I saw that girl before," I cried.

"Where?" George asked. I told them about my dream. Mom understood it more than George did. I cried and cried.

My 11th BiRthDay...

We had celebrated my birthday earlier the same way it had been every single year. Except for one thing. I saw Analise again. Only briefly. I saw her out the window, but she ran. I had promised myself to avoid being alone at all costs. But of course, I get stuck in an alone situation.

"Polly! Stay home for two minutes! I'm going to pick up George from his card game. Do you want me to take or leave Little Sky?" Mom shouted up the steps.

"Can I come?" I asked.

"Fine my little 11 year old!" Mom said as I walked down the steps. She gave me a hug and we piled into the car. We drove along for about a minute before arriving at a small rickety old house. Mom went inside to pick up George. I started hearing voices and noises besides the soft breaths of my brother sleeping. I slumped down in my seat.

"Polly," someone said and I jumped up. Analise was sitting in the front seat talking to me. I opened my mouth and tried to scream, but nothing came out.

"I'm not here to hurt you. I'm trying to tell you something. Polly, I'm trying to tell you something. Do not be afraid. I'm here to protect you. I lived on this earth before you. I used to play piano. I had come from-." Mom walked up to the car with George and Analise was gone.

I was breathing deeply. Mom and George asked what was wrong. I shook my head and said "Nothing."

That night I couldn't sleep. I lay in bed thinking.

I wonder if Mom remembers what I told her about me. I wonder if she cares. I hope Analise doesn't come again...wait, yes I do. Wait, I don't know. I wish I knew what is happening. I want her to finish what she was saying.... I thought before falling asleep.

I had another dream. This one was different than

other dreams. This one was a murder mystery. Not scary, but funny. Before I woke up, I saw a really bright light and Analise came. This time was different. I wasn't scared. Analise talked to me without having to tell me to calm down. We actually had a conversation. She told me about her life and who she was. She told me about what things meant. The most important thing was that she told me about me. I discovered something I would never have learned without her telling me.

"Remember that always, Polly," Analise smiled, "I have to go. I'll visit you again soon."

She left and I woke up. I was happy now. I never told anyone what she said and I never will. Nobody had to know but me.

CHAPTER**TWELVE**

Sixth and seventh grade were hard, but Icky Nicky wasn't there! She transferred to some school miles and miles away.

Eighth grade was the year where a lot of new things started. Mom kept saying "I can't believe you're 13 already!" and Little Sky started school. I had not seen Analise again after my 11th birthday and I still hadn't forgotten about Skylar. I would still play with his ring, which now hung, around my neck on a chain.

Andy's brother had gotten married and now Andy was going to become an aunt. The bad was still here. Mom was now in the hospital. She had been there a shirt while, and the doctor's said she was doing well. I hoped she could come home soon. George wouldn't get out of bed and wouldn't stop crying. I spent most afternoons at Andy's during this time. Andy had a boyfriend for two months named Justin. He was only two weeks older than she. He was nice, but not someone I would like. Andy wouldn't stop trying to convince me to go out with a guy named Derrick, who liked me, but I kept saying no. He was kind of cute, but I only liked him as a friend and I wondered how any guy would like me in the first place, which totally blows all self-confidence. That year there was a big dance and I promised Andy I'd go with Derrick. He was really nice. He was one of my best friends in a way. Like, my guy best friend.

It was about the 3rd week of school when we were standing by the lockers.

"Are you going to Kacy's party?" Derrick asked us.

"Nope. Never was. I hate that girl. She's so annoying!" I said grabbing my social studies book.

"I'm going with Justin," Andy said. Her hair was a bit shorter now.

"Will you go with me?" Derrick asked batting his eyelashes.

"No, Derrick. I told you already. I only like you as a friend. F-R-I-E-N-D," I said rolling my eyes. I had more friends than just Andy that year. We had a little group. There was Emily, the popular girly girl one, and Derrick the active funny one. There was Kate, the sporty one, and Jessica the gorgeous but quiet (and may I mention food addict) one. There was also Justin and Kaleb, the stupid ones. Then there was River, the smart one who didn't date, but wasn't gay either like Jon. Jon was the gay one. Last but not least, were Andy and I. The ten of us hung out together as one big group. Nina, JJ, Jason, and Brittany were four people in our school who most of us hated, but they weren't mean to us in particular. Just people in general. Any popular people, like Emily and Jessica, they stayed away from. It was very beneficial having popular people as friends. All my friends knew about Skylar and about my mom being sick. They were very supportive. We all stood up for each other and barely ever fought which was definitely a good thing.

"So do you miss him?" Derrick asked holding my

necklace/ ring in his hand. I blushed.

"I'm not going to the dance you guys," I said taking the necklace out of his hands.

"Really?" he asked.

"Yea."

"Please come!" Andy insisted.

"No."

"You are very weird," Emily said as she finished putting on lipstick. Jessica came over talking to Jon and Kaleb.

"I've known this girl since I was like five and trust me, she's been weirder, but that's not an excuse not to go," Andy said. Across the hall, River was talking to a girl from our Spanish class. He blushed and laughed. When he was done talking to her he came over to us.

"River has a girl friend. You do know that's totally against the rules," Jon said.

"Does not. She's just a friend. And since when are there rules?" River asked as the girl walked away.

"River. You know you like her. You flirt with her like every day," Jon said.

"Cut it out. Let's leave River and his 'friend' alone," I said using air quotes with 'friend.'

"Thanks Pol," River said half sarcastically.

This was a typical 8th grade day for our odd and diverse group.

The DaY of the dAnce...

"Oh my gosh!" I said to myself as a limo parked in front of my house. Derrick and Andy stepped out.

"Everyone's inside. Let's go!" They said trying to pull me in.

"No! I'm not going," I said trying to warm up.

"Jon decided to go," Derrick said.

"And I didn't. I'll be on the computer and stuff. IM

through your cell if you get bored," I said walking back inside.

"Party pooper!" Andy yelled laughing.

Later ThAt NiGhT...

I was playing video games when an IM popped up on my window and killed my video game dude. IM GOING TO UR HOUSE NOW. U SHLDV CME W/ DERRICK!! BUT I PITY U SO IM COMING.XOX ANDY. A little while later the doorbell rang. I opened it and Andy and River came inside. River was covered in punch. I laughed at him.☺

"Why are *you* here? And what happened?" I asked River.

"Fell into the punch bowl," he shrugged.

"Ha. Right. You mean Nina *pushed* you into the punch table when you asked her to dance," Andy laughed. She picked a piece of sushi off the back of his shirt.

"He even comes with food!" she exclaimed popping it into her mouth.

"Um ew! Go shower River!" I laughed and asked where Justin was. It was unusual for Andy to be around without Justin nowadays.

"Oh, I broke up with him."

"What? Why?" I asked. I wondered why she said it so casually.

"I felt like it," she said. I could tell she was lying. I told River he could use the shower and when I heard the shower upstairs come on, signaling River couldn't hear, I poked Andy and said, "You're lying. When he gets out of the shower, he'll tell me the truth."

"He doesn't know anything," she snapped.

"Tell me," I said, "I'm your best friend."

"Fine. I didn't break up with him. He broke up with

me," she sighed. Tears filled her eyes. "He said we were destined to be friends and that it would never have worked out anyway. He said he likes another girl."

"I hate boys," I said.

"Me too," She agreed as her tears slowly dried.

"WHAT AM I SUPPOSED TO WEAR?" River yelled down the steps.

"I DUNNO. BORROW GEORGE'S CLOTHES," I yelled back.

"They'll fit perfect," Andy said sarcastically. "Are you ever going to date Derrick? You guys are perfect. Kate and Jessica are just stupid and think Skylar is the one but trust me, you need Derrick."

George came up from the basement. I had forgotten that he was here. He still looked just like Andy. I wondered if maybe George really was Andy's dad. That would be so cool. We would be, like, stepsisters.

"Hey, girls," He said.

"Hi George!" we said nervously.

"Just came up to get some popcorn. Mets are winning! This is going to be a good game," he said.

"CALL MY MOM! SHE COULD BRING SOME CLOTHES OVER. GEORGE'S DON'T FIT!" River yelled. I cringed. I wasn't supposed to have any boys over past 9 o'clock.

"Who was that? And why does he need clothes?" George asked. Wow. That really sounded suspicious.

"The TV," I said.

"No," Andy and George said at the same time. Only when Andy said it, it was more a no as in 'No this can't be happening'. George went upstairs slowly. Andy picked up the cordless and dialed River's number as fast as she could. He picked up on the second ring.

"Hurry up! Hide! Hide!" Andy yelled into the phone, "Don't ask why! Are you hiding? Good. Bye."

She hung up.

"So about you and Derrick," she said leaning on the wall.

"No."

"C'mon. Just date him for a few weeks. Please!" she begged. I rolled my eyes.

"Never. Not in a million years. By the way, you really got over Justin fast," I said changing the subject.

"Yup," she said even though I could see sadness in her eyes, "I'm just good with those things."

Just then River came stumbling down the stairs quickly with only a towel wrapped around his waist, his clothes and phone under his arm.

"Sorry guys! Gotta run!" River scurried out the door just barely having time to shout out to us. We laughed hysterically, but silence came upon us when George stomped down the steps.

"Remember we set a rule no boys after nine?" George asked.

"Yeah," I looked at my feet.

"What time is it?" he asked.

I looked around.

"Time to go to bed." I tried to escape to my room, but George's evil eye stopped me.

"Don't try to act smart, Polly." George's glare was like that of stone. "Why was that boy here at......11?"

"He's just River, George. My friend. I didn't even know he was coming. Andy came over and River kind of tagged along 'cuz he got punch spilled all over him and he wanted to take a shower. Yeah," I said quickly. I expected George to say something like *That's no excuse! You're grounded for a month!* But he didn't. His response was quite surprising, actually.

"Really?" he asked seriously.

"Swear," I responded.

"Ok." He shrugged his shoulders and acted like nothing happened. I sighed with relief.

"You do know why your mother and I don't want boys over past nine right?"

"Not really, but I'm sure we don't want to," Andy answered for me. I nodded in agreement.

"Ok," he said calmly.

MoNdAy at schOol...

Derrick came up to me and said, "Polly, will you go with me to the movies Saturday?"

"No. Derrick, seriously. You have to understand that we are just friends," I said.

"Please, Polly. I'll give up if you say no," Derrick begged, but he didn't sound like he was really trying to convince me anymore.

"Derrick, No. I'm sorry. Besides, if you give up you won't be obsessed with me anymore so give up. Go out with Rebecca or something. She really likes you," I said.

"Ok. Fine then. I will," Derrick walked away and over to Rebecca just like that. I stared at them. I was kind of happy that we were just friends now and that he got over everything, but I was a bit worried. I have no idea why.

"What's up?" I asked sitting down for lunch. I noticed that Andy was pretending to read a book, but really looking over the top of it and watching Justin with his new girl friend. She was gorgeous. I was happy for Justin that he found this girl, but mad that he left Andy.

"I have the most amazing things to tell you!" Kate

said all bubbly, distracting me from my train of thought.

"Go," I said examining what seemed to be potato salad before eating it.

"It's about a guy," Kate said pulling her tray away from Jessica and Kaleb who were about to dive for her brownie.

"Ok," Kate smiled, "This really cute ninth grader asked me on a date",

"Big deal. I hate boys," I said even though I knew she couldn't hear me because she was too busy answering questions for Emily who was ecstatic about the whole thing. Emily acted like a normal not rich 13 year old would act if someone randomly gave them a trillion dollars. I could only imagine what she would've acted like if a ninth grader asked *her* out instead of Kate. River stood up and backed away from the table to answer a cell phone call and Jessica poked Andy trying to see what she was staring at.

All of a sudden Jessica screamed, "Oh. My. Gosh. You're staring at Justin again aren't you?"

Justin turned around and waved. Then he got back to his girlfriend. I walked over to Justin. Andy was freaking out because she didn't want me to go over there.

"Were you cheating on Andy?" I asked interrupting his make out session.

"I'm kind of busy here," he said gesturing to his girl-friend.

"Yea, yea. She's cute. Listen up; you stay away from me, Andy, and any of the rest of us. Nobody hurts my friend like that," I said to him. Then I kicked him and got surprised at him saying "ow!" Then I walked away. He took his girlfriends hand and left the cafeteria.

I smiled satisfied with myself even though I did practically nothing. Justin was a wimp. I didn't even kick hard.

"So where were we?" I asked taking a last glance at Derrick.

OnE weEk latEr...

"Everyone's going out with somebody except me," I said plopping down on my bed. Andy had just come to my house after going to the movies with her new boyfriend. I invited some other friends, too, for a sleep over.

"It's ok," Kate said smiling.

"Yeah. There is someone there for you," Emily smiled.

"I think you should track down Skylar," Jessica said pulling out a movie from my bookcase.

"You could've had Derrick, but no. You just had to say no," Andy sighed.

Emily had been showing us pictures from her double date, her and her boyfriend with Jessica and her date, at Coney Island. I wished I had a boyfriend.

"At least you know it's worse for Jon. He's just gay," Kate said stealing popcorn from Andy.

"I do feel bad for you. You have no boyfriend, your mom is in the hospital, you lost your chance with Derrick and now you're jealous--," Emily started to say. I triggered back at the word jealous.

"I am not jealous!" I said sitting up. Everybody stood still and the only sound was Jessica munching on popcorn. We all burst out laughing. Silence made us laugh all the time.

"But I'm seriously NOT jealous," I said leaning back on a pillow.

"Yes you are," Emily said laughing out her last giggles.

"I bet she's not. She never liked him." Kate started to talk, but was interrupted from a nudge by Emily signaling for her to shut up and go along with it.

"Admit it," Jessica said filing her nails.

"We'll force it out of her," Emily whispered to Jessica. Jessica nodded. They all stared at me in silence. Jessica and Kate tried to hold in giggles, and Andy read a magazine using it as a way to keep from laughing. But as for Emily? She was good at hiding her laughs when she wanted to.

"PUH-LESE! I would never in a million years like him," I said smiling shyly.

"Aw," Everyone sighed disappointed.

"I don't even know why he liked me! I'm not pretty," I said looking down at my feet.

"NOT PRETTY?" Emily asked surprised. "NOT PRETTY? Girl, take a look in the mirror you're gorgeous."

"No I'm not," I shook my head as Emily and Jessica tried pushing me over to the mirror.

"You need self confidence. Look in that mirror and think about how your life would have changed if you had confidence then you'll see yourself and think 'Who is that beautiful celebrity?" Emily said.

I sat down in front of the mirror and stared at myself for a long time. I didn't see me. For some reason I saw different people saying different things. I saw Emily talking about beauty, Skylar talking to me right before he left, Analise, and even the Devil sending me on my mission. The Devil's face in this picture was different. Everything around me blocked out. I listened to all these people as my thoughts came together. Suddenly they all fell apart again without me even having time to take note of what these thoughts actually were. I now saw myself with my hair pulled back in a high ponytail with my plaid pajama pants and a tank top and bunny slippers like I had been wearing that very moment. I looked into my own eyes and my brain began to hurt. I saw what I didn't think I'd see. I thought I'd see an ugly girl looking at herself in the mirror, but instead I saw my thoughts get put together and fall apart again within seconds. I reached my hand out and touched where my cheek was in my reflection. I forced a smile, although sad that I almost knew what my life was all about, and lost the answer. "Yea," I said, "I guess you're right for once," We laughed and had a pillow fight.

ThE nExt daY At tHe hOsPitaL...

"Hi, mom," I sighed sitting down next to her. She looked horrible.

"Hey, Polly!" she said trying to sound enthusiastic. But her voice was very weak. We sat in silence for a moment. I couldn't think of what to say. Mom kept on smiling. I finally cracked a small smile and asked why she was smiling.

"Because I have great news," she said softly.

"What?" I asked suddenly excited.

"First off, I got you something or, I asked my friend to pick it up for you because, as you know, I can't really leave." She reached into a bag and pulled out a small emerald green notebook with little jewels on it.

"You've always liked writing and I think you may have told me about wanting to be an author," she explained as I stared with awe. I did enjoy writing sometimes, but couldn't recall telling anyone. I have no idea how she knew, but moms know everything. "But I've never seen you write a story unless you were complaining about something you had to write for school. And school doesn't really count anyway. I got you that so you could practice more of your writing that you've always wanted to do."

I held the notebook as if she had told me, "If you drop it the world will end," It was gorgeous and so special to me.

"Oh my gosh! Thank you so much, Mom!" I said leaning forward to hug her.

"That's not even the best part," she said into my hair.

"What?" I asked smiling a big smile.

"I'm coming home soon",

"AHHH!!!!" I practically yelled this. I hugged her and kissed her. I couldn't believe it.

ONe WeEk LaTeR...

Mom walked inside slowly wearing a bandana around her baldhead and looking a bit tired. Little Sky ran and hugged her leg. He looked up at her and smiled.

"Mommy!" he cheered. She smiled. George came to give her a kiss then led her to the couch where she could sit to greet everyone. Aunt Malinda and Andy's family were both on their way over. Andy and I had already been at my house waiting. We cheered and giggled.

I went over to kiss her.

"How are you feeling?" Andy asked.

"Better," Mom said looking around and smiling, "Oh, I missed this house. I missed being home."

I was so happy she was going to be all right. Everyone sat in silence for a moment.

"How's everything going? Do you guys have boyfriends?" Mom asked breaking the silence.

I blushed and lightly nudged Andy signaling not to

bring up anything. "No."

"I want something to eat," Mom said as the door-bell rang.

"1 sec," I said running to the door.

"Hi, Polly!" Aunt Malinda said in her peppy voice. Aunt Malinda kissed my cheek and squealed as she walked in to meet everyone else.

"Well," I said, "Let's do something."

CHAPTER**THIRTEEN**

ONe month LaTeR...

Andy and I stepped over to the door ever so slowly; River and Emily following close behind.

"Tell me again why we're doing this?" Emily's voice floated into the darkness.

"Because. I lost a bet. Now I have to go down there and get the stuff for the prank I have to play on the teacher," I wasn't lying. Jon bet me that I couldn't go one day without doodling on my notebook. If I lost I had to pull an extreme prank on one of the teachers and get all my supplies from the basement of the school which had a famous legend to go along with it about a creepy murderer who lived down there. You guessed it. I lost. Now I had to go get some supplies from the school's outdoor basement thing. I was too scared to go alone. I didn't believe the legend, but I was still scared.

"OK," I said leaning down to open the door. I held onto the railing, "Who's coming with me?"

"I just got my hair done," Emily said shaking her head fiercely.

"Me too," Jon said scratching the back of his neck. Andy giggled.

"I'll go. It's just a stupid legend," Andy shrugged and followed me close behind.

"You staying up alone?" I asked turning to Emily and Jon. They turned to each other and Emily sighed, reluctantly following. Jon looked around and ran to catch up.

As soon as we were all at the bottom of the stairs, the doors shut. Emily screamed and Jon ran to try and open it.

"OH MY GOD!!" I screamed. I was freaked out. I didn't hear a response as the lights went out.

"Hello?" I asked shaking, "Are you guys there?" I heard no answer. I was so scared. I heard the door open, then some shouting, and then the door shut again. In the distance I heard Andy yelling, "Polly where are you? Are you still down there?"

"I'm down here!" I yelled. I was pretty sure I was crying at this point. I tried to yell again, but nothing came out of my mouth. I opened my mouth again, but a large hand covered it and pulled me back into the darkness.

The neXt MorNing...

I opened my eyes. I was really cold. I breathed out and turned to the side. I was lying under a blanket outside the basement doors. I couldn't remember a thing except the shouting. I sat up cautiously. I felt vibrating and jumped. I looked at my sweatshirt. I had forgotten about my cell phone. I picked it up and answered not caring who it was.

"Hello?" I said in a small voice.

"Polly? Where are you? I've been calling you since last night! We've been looking everywhere! I called the police, I talked to your friends, and they can't find Andy, Emily, or Jon either!" Mom said.

"I need help. I don't know what happened, but I'm at the school we were going to get supplies," My voice trailed off and I cried.

"Don't worry, George is coming to get you now," Mom said worried. She sounded like she was crying too.

I sat for a few minutes before I heard footsteps and I turned around quickly. George came and he was speechless. He picked me up and hugged me tight.

"Let's go," he said.

Before I knew it, I was home and my mom and brother were kissing me a lot. George put me on my bed and I fell asleep.

When I finally woke up I got dressed and went downstairs.

"Polly!" Mom said. She hugged me. A cop came out from the kitchen.

"Is this one of the victims?" he asked George.

"This is Polly," George said nodding. I shook his hand and went to sit down on the couch with them.

"Why were you and your friends down their last night?" the cop asked.

"We lost a bet and we needed something from the basement," I told the cop. To my surprise, he didn't give me any speeches on not going out at night like that or anything. I guess he was too busy interrogating to do that.

"What happened?" the cop asked. I told him the whole entire story with every detail I could think of and even more, that I didn't really remember, but for some reason I knew it happened.

"Do you have any idea where your friends are?" he asked.

"I would've thought they went home?" I asked suddenly worried.

"No. We can't find them. Your friends," he looked

down at his list, "Emily and Jon."

"What about Andy?" I asked.

"Oh, we found her. She will be ok, but she was in shock during what ever happened and can't remember anything."

I gasped. "She'll be ok, right?"

"I said yes. She will be fine."

"Can I see her?" I asked sitting up.

"No. Not right now. Where do you think your friends might have gone?"

"I don't know," I said sinking into my seat.

I rested for the next few days. Or, that's what Mom and George called it. Resting. To me, it was anything but resting. I was worried about all of my friends. Even the ones who hadn't been there. I had no time to rest for even a second and I barely slept. I called River, Andy, Kate, Emily, and Jon, but nobody picked up their cells. Then I tried Jessica, Kaleb, and Derrick. Still nobody. One or Two weeks later, I started getting phone calls from everyone. Including the police. They wanted me down at the station again. They had found Emily and Jon.

At tHe StAtioN...

"Where are they? Can I see them?" I asked running into the station quickly.

"I don't think you want to," one of the police said. My face fell.

"Why?" I asked looking around.

"Polly," one said kneeling to be at my height, "We found your friends, but they're not alive."

At first I didn't understand and I couldn't think straight. Then it all came to me. Emily and Jon were dead.

I burst into tears. Two of my friends were dead. I couldn't help but cry even in front of all these strangers. I cried and cried and cried.

OnE mOntH laTer...

I looked at the newspaper that was lying on the table. They had found the guy who killed Emily and Jon. The rumor was true. It was all over the news. This guy was going to jail for life. He had murdered many children before. Many unsolved cases were now solved and they all led to this one guy who had snuck into the school's basement 5 years before. Mom explained to me the horrible things that happened. The guy took all of us, but Andy managed to escape. The man was mentally challenged and needed to kill kids because he had weird dreams telling him to. Nobody knew why I'd been spared.

"Polly," Mom told me, "You just weren't meant to die yet. There is still something you have to do on this Earth."

In school all the kids would ask Andy and me, "Are you OK? Are you OK?" But we never responded. It was seemingly pointless.

I walked through the halls of school silently next to Andy. I was a lot quieter than I used to be. So was everyone else. Or maybe that was just when I was around. I cried a lot more. I was scared. Everywhere I turned I was afraid someone would pop out and kill me. I never went anywhere alone. Not even to the bathroom. I had someone come guard my stall, but even then I would be terrified until I got out. This is how my years passed by. Until high school. In the third year of high school, everything changed. That year, the whole past was behind me and nothing that was from the past affected me in any way... until Icky Nicky came to town. Suddenly my past mattered more than anything else.

CHAPTER**FOURTEEN**

ThiRd yEar oF hIgH schOol...

"I got it!" I cheered. I had gotten my learners permit and I was so excited. I wanted to go out and drive right that second.

"That's great! George can take you out and teach you how to drive," Mom said. Mom's cancer was in remission and she was looking much better.

"In a few minutes," George said. He was glued to the game. I hated watching sports, but watching sports was practically George's life these days.

"Now you can drive me to soccer practice," little Sky said pulling an apple out of the basket. He was older now, of course, and getting way involved in soccer, but besides that he hated other sports. He still did after school activities like choir and some kind of junior architect class or something. He loved to build things. Even with my books. Sometimes when I came home, I would see an Empire State Building or a Leaning Tower of Pisa built out of books. My books.

"Um no," I said laughing.

"Give your brother a break," Mom said. I rolled my eyes and stuck my tongue at him playfully. Suddenly John Mayer's "Waiting on the World to Change," started playing. I pulled out my cell. It was Matt. He was my boyfriend at the time.

"Hey!" I said picking it up and walking up to my room.

"Hey!" Little Sky mimicked. He hated Matt."Hi, Polls!" Matt said. "How'd it go?"

"I got my learner's permit!" I squealed.

"I guess that means I can't drive you everywhere anymore."

"Aw, you could still drive me everywhere if you want to."

"No it's ok. You need the practice."

I talked to him for a while and played with my necklace.

"Polly. Get off the phone," Mom yelled up the stairs.

"OK, Mom!" I said my good-byes to Matt and I went downstairs. I would see him at school anyway.

ScHoOl...

I said hi to all my friends and met up with Andy. Everything was going fine until 3ʳᵈ period when I met my worst nightmare.

"Hi Polly! I haven't seen you in so long!" I turned around to see Icky Nicky staring at me.

"I'm glad," I said.

"Aw. That's not nice," Icky Nick said in a voice that was totally fake. "I came here just to see you."

"Right," I mumbled. This was a horrible encounter.

"How's your life going?" she asked waving to one of her passing friends. "Mine is better than yours as usual. I'm dating the cutest boy in school and I just got here. Also, Daddy owns his own hotels and we have lot's of money now",

"You do realize how much you suck at being

mean," I said.

"No," Icky Nicky said pouting. "I'm always nice to you." She turned and walked down the hall. I wanted to brag to her saying how the cutest boy in school just happened to be a jerk who was arrested three times and my boyfriend was way nicer, but she wasn't worth it. She would probably try to steal Matt anyway, and she could. She had the ability to steal any guy from any girl unless the guy was real smart like Skylar.

I caught up with Andy and explained exactly what happened. She freaked out.

"Oh my god!" she said. "We have to transfer immediately! I hate her! She's so annoying",

"Relax. She's bad at being mean anyway remember? We can stand up to her, I think," I said.

"Ok. Calm Andy. Calm. But seriously, why does she even bother with us? Why does she hate us?" Andy would have gone on if I didn't interrupt her.

"Because I stopped her from making fun of back-stabbing Arey," I was trying to do this calmly. Andy had been very, VERY moody lately and this wasn't even bad. She wasn't doing so well at home either. Her parents were going through a divorce and so was her brother. Her brother had been drinking too much and his wife kicked him out. He now lived at their mom's house. Andy's mom's boyfriend was always pressuring Andy about school and her mom did the same to her just because she wanted to agree with this guy on child care in case they got married or something. Home was about the worst place for her to be so she began spending almost all her time at my house.

"Are you all right?" I asked.

"Yea. It's just my life is already crappy and this girl adds so much to it. She's not mean just annoying and people think she's mean. She ruins people's lives and relationships because she was unfortunately born to be disgustingly beautiful," he sighed.

"You don't know the half of it. Your life is the best thing that could happen to a person compared to what happens in my life. I've been having tragedies since I was a baby. Remember?" I said. We walked down the hallway to the lockers where we would meet up with Matt. Andy hated Matt. Matt's brother used to date Andy, but Matt convinced him Andy was no good so they broke up. That caused a short period of not speaking between Matt and me, but it was nothing. We went back together after a while. Andy told me it was all right. I started to wonder why everyone hated Matt.

"Hi, Matt," I said. As soon as I said it, Andy turned down the hall. She avoided Matt at all costs.

"Hi," he said his eyes following her as she walked down the hall.

"We need to talk," Matt said. I knew this wasn't good.

"Break up?" I asked knowingly.

"I'm sorry, Polly, but there's this new girl and I think I have a chance-," he began.

"Oh my gosh. I can't believe this. I should've known. Just don't come crying to me when she doesn't go for you." I walked away without letting him respond. I found myself doing that a lot lately. Walking away before people could respond.

At HoMe...

"Hi," I said when I opened the door and saw Andy.

"Hey," she said. There were round black patches under her eyes. She hadn't looked like that earlier.

"What's up?" I asked.

"Listen, can I stay here for a couple of weeks?" she asked without even looking at me or explaining herself.

"Um...yea. That's fine," I said. I watched as she walked in and went upstairs. Probably to the guest room.

I walked back to the table and sat down for dinner.

"What's up with Andy?" Little Sky asked. I just shook my head and continued to eat.

THe NeXt DaY...

"Hi," I said when Andy came down. We were the only two awake. It was 6 am.

"What's wrong?" I asked as she sat down.

"My mom's boyfriend has got problems." Her voice was quiet.

"What kind?"

"He hits."

"What?" I was scared for her.

"He hits." She obviously wanted to end the conversation there, but I wouldn't let her.

"Did he hit you?"

"And kicked me out of the house. He hit Mom too because she told him I couldn't leave."

"Why?"

"I got a "C" on my math test. He's mentally retarded. I hate him. It seems like nobody in my family has respect for themselves or others. It's a bad influence on me. It seems like I'm the only one in my family who can actually control my life properly. My brother gets married to a girl who has no education and to me is mentally insane and then loses his wife because he drinks too much, then my mom dates an

118

abusive man while in the middle of a divorce with my dad who has no job and no money and is going home to live with his parents, like my brother is doing. Before you know it, Mom's boyfriend will marry her, kill her, and get custody of me, then my dad will never want to see anyone of us again (he already doesn't want to see us) and me and my brother will become suicidal. Story of my new and horrid life."

"I didn't expect that much out of you."

"Yea well you got what you asked for."

"I guess I did," I said leaning back in my chair. "You can't run away from your problems, Andy. You have to-"

"Geez! Polly. Polly, Polly, Polly. Stop talking like my mom. Or not my mom, but how most moms, well you know what I mean. I can't even believe you. You know I never listen to any of that. I bet I'm going to grow up like my parents and brother if I don't die first. Face it, Polly. I won't be a good kid. Too many bad influences. Life sucks if it's like mine." She stood up and grabbed her jacket.

"Where are you going?"

"Out."

"Where?"

"Somewhere where a girl by the name of Polly won't nag me with questions," she walked out the door and down the sidewalk. She was walking towards the park. I wondered why. I put on my coat and followed at a safe distance.

I had been right. She walked right into the park, but she didn't stay there. She walked through it towards a bridge. It wasn't crowded at this time of day. Just the occasional car.

"Where are you going?" I asked stopping in my tracks.

"Over there," she said. She didn't look at me, stop, or point at anything. Just continued walking. I decided to catch up, clueless of whatever was going to happen next.

"What? Where?"

She walked up to the side of the bridge.

"Here," she said actually turning to me this time. Then it hit me.

"Andy, you don't want to do this!" I gasped.

"How would you know?" she said taking off her jacket, "You never went through this much pressure."

"Yes, Andy, I have. But this isn't how you solve this kind of thing."

"Or is it?" she said this more like a statement than a question.

"You know, life is about the biggest challenge you could ever take on and suicide is like backing down from that challenge. It's like saying 'I loose' and I want to quit the game. No matter what happens, you should play the game to the end. In the end, after you get through it, you'll find that the prize will be all worth it. The Andy I know wouldn't back down from any challenge," I said. Neither of us spoke for a minute.

"Polly," Andy smiled, "That was one of the most meaningful and important things you've ever said to me. Also the weirdest and most random."

I watched as she picked up her coat and started down the path again.

"I have to go talk to my family," she said. I smiled, not really realizing what I said till moments later. I thought of it as a perfect thing to say.

The nExt daY...

"So I've decided, if it's ok, that instead of going

with them, I could stay here with you," Andy said. After talking to her mom, she knew her parents were getting divorced and her mom was moving in with her boyfriend. I had always thought her family was so stable. I guess some things can change that easily.

I stuck my lip out and made a puppy face to Mom and George. They smiled and nodded. Andy and I screamed! We were overjoyed! We would be kind of like sisters.

At dinner that night, Mom and George asked about how Andy's family used to be and about her extended family and stuff. As soon as George heard Andy's mom's maiden name, he was silent for a minute staring at Andy.

"I think I'm going to go watch TV," he said still staring at her. Everyone knew something was wrong. It was obvious.

"What did I do?" Andy asked.

"Nothing. You didn't do anything. I just need to talk to him," Mom said getting up from the table. Of course, Andy and I hid in the next room listening. Mom was talking about how he could always be honest with her and he could tell her anything. Same kind of stuff she gave me except in a husband wife kind of way. Then I heard George's voice lower.

"It was a long time ago," he started as I strained my ears to hear. "Long before we were dating, I had this girl friend. One day, she got pregnant." George sounded sad, "She named the baby Andrea, and Andy for short."

Andy and I looked at each other and gasped.

"George is my dad," Andy whispered.

"But wouldn't that mean he was your brother's dad too?" I asked.

"I don't know. Maybe my mom didn't tell him she

was married or something like that," Andy began, "and they broke up when he found out?"

"Yes. That's how it happened." Andy and I looked up as George and Mom stood over us. I knew they were listening. Andy stood up, and George hugged her. For a second Andy just stood there, but then she hugged back. Like father like daughter. I always knew they were alike, but I have to admit this was kind of random.

I hadn't noticed till a few minutes later that this meant Andy was my stepsister. There was this long court case and Andy wound up coming to live with us and her mom's boyfriend was charged with physical and verbal abuse. It was an almost, but not quite happily ever after. There were still lots more life to live.

My 17th BirThdAy...

"Happy Birthday!" everyone said. To me, it didn't feel happy. I didn't know why, but something didn't feel right. The party ended a little earlier than it was supposed to because I said I didn't feel good. I lie on my bed thinking. *What's wrong?* I thought.

"Hey. Can I come in?" Andy asked.

"Sure." I turned to the side and stared at the wall.

"What's up?" she sat down next to me.

"I don't know." I shook my head slowly.

"Maybe it's...like...pressure? Ya know, because you'll be starting college soon or something like that," she suggested.

"I don't think so," I sighed. "I'll figure it out eventually."

Andy smiled. "Tomorrow we're going to visit a couple of colleges nearby. We'll see if we like any of them."

"Ok," I said. Andy left and I started thinking again

and didn't notice myself falling asleep.

"Hi, Polly! Long time no see!" I turned and smiled.

"Hi!" I said to Analise.

"Oh, I almost forgot, Happy Birthday!" she said as we started to walk.

"Thanks, but it hasn't been that much fun. I don't know what's wrong," I sighed.

"Yea," she looked up at the sky, "I remember some birthdays I felt that way too."

"Did you figure out what it was?" I asked. Analise looked so much older now. Like she was growing up with me somehow even though she died.

"Yeah. It's not that big of a deal. Sometimes you're just not in the birthday mood. Let's say there is some big test or something like that going on. Then that wouldn't put you in the birthday mood."

"Oh. I personally thought it would be a big thing that you would give me a bunch of advice on." I giggled a little.

"No. That's with only certain special things," Analise said.

"So why'd you pick now to come see me?" I asked.

"I don't know. I felt it was about time. I haven't seen you in a while. And I think that you're going to need me. I heard you got a new step sister," she turned to me, her eyes twinkling.

"Yeah. Andy. I kind of liked it better when we were just friends not step sisters. I don't know why. I think it's just a little too close."

"OK. I understand that. What college do you want to go to?" she asked.

"NYU. I heard it's a pretty good writing school."

"I know you like writing, but you don't do it that much. Maybe you should try getting into it more."

"I guess I should," I knew she was right about that, "I'll start writing when I leave this place. Where are we anyway?"

"I'm not sure. I think some type of gardens from the looks of it."

"It's pretty nice."

"Wanna know something?" she smiled.

"What?"

"Skylar is attending college at NYU. "

"Really?" I got something in my eye and started to blink. Then I was in my room again. It was dark. I turned on the lights and looked at the clock. It was about 2AM. I didn't care. I grabbed a notebook and started to write. I kept writing for hours not even knowing what I was writing about until about 8AM when I finally got to read it. I loved it. I had written a story about my life, and I thought that was one of the most perfect ideas. *People would read this!* I thought. My stomach growled and nobody was awake yet. I went into the kitchen and slipped some breakfast into the toaster. While I was waiting for it to finish I turned and stared at the unfinished story. 'Polly Wood', I scribbled across the top. That's what I would call my story.

THe FoLlOwInG WeEk....

"I loved your book!" Andy said stepping onto the porch.

"I still want to go to NYU," I said.

"But Princeton is so much better and I want to go to college with you!" Andy sighed, "It's so unfair."

"We would still see each other. It's ok," I smiled.

"Yeah, but not as much."

"Well, tonight I'm going down to NYU to see it. I'm also going to stay overnight because it'll be too late to come home," I said.

"No you're not."

"Yes I am. Mom said it was ok, but only for one night."

"I'll be all alone tonight?" Andy gasped.

"Relax. It's going to be fine. You'll have Little Sky and Mom and George."

"I might bring you back some souvenirs from Wicked," I grinned.

"No fair! I want to come too!"

"Ha and ha." Andy punched my arm so I punched her back and we laughed hysterically. You're probably thinking, "Well, what's so funny about that? Or anything else the book says you laughed at?" I would probably think that too. But you had to be in the moment to see the humor. So shut up.

The nExT daY...

I walked into the college and looked around. It looked nice.

"Um, do you know where the dorms are?" a girl asked me.

"No. I don't go to college here. I'm just looking because I might come next year.

"Me, too."

"Ok. We can help each other out I guess." I smiled, "Oh, my name's Polly. Polly Brooks."

"I'm Carolyn Aden." That girl soon became one of my greatest friends. Carolyn was one of those people who are impossible to argue with because she couldn't make anyone mad. She was the kind of person with a great, but indescribable personality. A great friend who is as trustworthy as trustworthy gets. By the end of that day, it had felt as if we had been friends since we were younger. We took down each other's screen names, e-mails, phone numbers, and addresses. She lived all the way in Rockville Centre, but I knew I'd see her again in college. You're probably wondering how I can learn this much about a person in just one day. Well, that's a good question that I honestly don't know the answer to. I know I was right about Carolyn thought. Oh, and she came with me to see Wicked and it was amazing!

FirSt WEek of SumMer...

I scanned the mail that lay across the table. There were a lot of letters. Many for Mom and George, and one for me. Andy had gotten her acceptance letter to Princeton two days earlier before and she started packing even though she didn't start for a while. I slowly opened the letter from NYU. I squeezed my eyes shut and unfolded the letter. I opened my eyes and as soon as I saw the first nine words, I knew I didn't make it. I cried for a second before Little Sky handed me another letter from NYU that said I made it. I screamed, too happy to get mad at Sky for making a fake rejection letter instead of giving me my acceptance letter.

"I made it! I made it!" I skipped around the house cheering. I called Carolyn to find out that we both made it! I was so happy. That night, we all went out to dinner like we had when Andy got accepted to Princeton. In a couple of months, I'd be 18 and going off to college at NYU with Carolyn. I couldn't wait.

CHAPTER**FIFTEEN**

Day bEfore thE firSt daY of CollEge...

"**A**ll settled in?" my parents asked me before leaving.

"Yeah." I liked my dorm a lot and wondered who my roommate would be. You know what? I'm going to forget the mystery. You probably already know that it's going to be Carolyn. Especially if you read like me and read the ending before the beginning.

I hugged Mom, George, and Little Sky.

"We'll miss you," Mom said holding me tight.

"I'll miss you too," I smiled. Then they left.

I set up a little more, placing my laptop on the desk, putting away some clothes. I got tired and laid down on my bed. I wondered what college would be like, and if I'd make friends. Just that moment, the door opened and Carolyn came in.

"Hi!" I smiled. I was so happy Carolyn was my roommate. I did not want some one else.

"Hi!" she said as I hugged her.

"How is it so far?" Carolyn asked.

"I have no idea. I haven't left the room yet. Hey, where are your parents? Mine wouldn't even leave."

"Oh. They couldn't come. They never come to anything from the least to the most important of things. I don't think they really care that much," she said as she started unpacking. I thought about what Analise had said about Skylar going to NYU. Could it be true?

A small white dog, I think an American Eskimo, suddenly hopped out of one of Carolyn's bags. I screamed, surprised.

"Shh! This is Atka. She's my dog, but I'm not sure if we are aloud to have dogs, but I had to take her. Don't tell anyone." Carolyn explained picking up Atka.

"She's so cute!" I said running over to pet her. I kind of wished I had a dog I could sneak into college.

A feW weEks laTer...

"Why do you of all people wind up following me wherever I go?" I said to Icky Nicky who I discovered was a classmate of mine.

"I don't know. It's not great for me either. You're not amusing at all. The only enjoyment I get out of you is how stupid you are and how low your fashion sense is. I don't see how we get stuck together. This doesn't work for me, this whole setup. Let me tell you one thing, stay away from all the guys and me. If you talk to any guy, he'll become too scared of girls to date me. Then again, just looking at me can transform them," she smiled.

"And you call *me* a dork." I walked away deciding not to bother with her. She wasn't worth it.

At lunchtime, I sat with Carolyn at a table in the middle.

"We're practically adults now, and Icky Nicky still hates me for doing who knows what when we were in kindergarten. I never imagined that she would follow me through life like this!" I explained.

"How rude!" Carolyn smiled and we laughed. She reached over for one of my Hershey Kisses and stole it successfully. It was just like Carolyn to do something like that. We fought playfully over the kiss for a while before the evil Icky Nicky approached our table.

"Um this is our table. Get up," she said.

"Um no," I said, "We were here first."

"So?" she tried pushing me out of my seat, but she barely moved me.

"What a wimp," I said sipping my soda.

"You don't call me a wimp, dork!" Icky Nicky said.

"Ha. Is that the best you've got?" I laughed.

"No. Wait and see." Icky Nicky smiled a wicked smile and walked off.

"I hate her. I hate her. I HATE HER!" I told Carolyn. "She's not even mean anymore! Just an over annoying burden added onto my life."

"Just ignore her. She must be about the stupidest person I know," she smiled and so did I. I knew Carolyn barely knew Icky Nicky at all, but she always made me feel better. It felt good to know there was someone beside myself who despised Icky Nicky. There was also Andy, but she wasn't there to comfort me and let us complain to each other about Icky Nicky. But I guess I was ok because I still had Carolyn. At least one of my best friends was with me. I couldn't imagine what it would be like if she wasn't there. I'd be all alone.

LateR tHat dAy...

"I have to do my science homework. Wish me luck." Carolyn stood up and took her notebook. She often did her homework in the library. Not a campus library, The New York City Public Library. You know, the one with the big lions in front?

"I'll come with you. I've never been there." I sat up.

"Ok." She smiled revealing a bunch of white teeth and a silver one in the back.

We took a cab to the library. We were never awake enough to walk anywhere besides places like class (where the option of taking a cab was unavailable). The cab passed a bunch of poor people.

"It must suck to be poor in America because most people help the poor in other countries. Not here," Carolyn sighed. I nodded in agreement. I had never thought of that before. Then I thought of myself and how I used to be one of them.

"What's the big library like?" I turned to her. I didn't feel like talking about the unfortunate.

"It's amazing! There are books all over and there are so many floors! Sometimes artist come to sketch sections of the library. It even has a gift shop. It is gorgeous!" her eyes twinkled as she described it and you could tell she loved it there.

I couldn't believe it! The place was huge! As I looked around, Carolyn went over to the lady at the front desk with bright red hair built up high. Carolyn giggled. I had to bite my tongue to keep from laughing.

Carolyn had to pull me away from the gift shop before we even started looking around. You can't blame me for loving gift shops! As we walked to another room, we passed through a giant hall with paintings on the walls, floors, and ceilings. I spun around in circles while looking up, suddenly thinking of a story idea. Carolyn laughed and told me I was acting kind of like a kid.

"I like being a kid," I smiled. We went over to a room that must've had over five thousand books and some computers. Carolyn guided me over to two computers and put her stuff down.

I walked over to a shelf with colorful books. I pulled a pink one out and flipped through the pages. It was a poetry book written in old English. I put it back on the shelf and walked up and down one side and across the hall towards some giant books that I struggled to carry around. I found the Guinness Book of World Records and looked at it. Soon Carolyn had finished, but I didn't notice. I just kept looking around, not noticing two pairs of eyes watching me. Carolyn laughed as I sang and ran my fingers quickly across the books on the shelves. It was then that I noticed a guy glancing at me before getting up from his seat by one of the computers. I looked and saw that the computer's screen saver was still on so he hadn't ever used the computer. I just decided to continue, and ignore him.

CHAPTER**SIXTEEN**

One yEar lateR...

"**I** got a B!" Carolyn said as she received the test.

"Me too!" we compared tests and put ourselves down for not getting some of the simple questions right. Later in the hall, everyone was talking about a party.

"Whose party?" I asked.

"That girl, Gina Calv-something."

"Is it a toga party? Because I despise toga parties," I asked.

"I have no idea," she said staring ahead.

"I know that look. You're looking at Mason again, aren't you?" Mason was a boy who Carolyn liked. I was pretty sure he liked her too, but neither one would talk to the other. Suddenly, Mason walked over with a nervous smile on his face.

"Um, hey, Carolyn," he said looking around with a pink face, "I was wondering if you...um...wanted to go to the party with me?"

"Yes! Yes! I'd love to!" Carolyn nodded quickly and a wide grin spread across her face. They exchanged some info and chatted a bit more.

After he finally walked away, I nudged her. She only giggled till we arrived to our next class.

A feW wEeks lAter...
"I can't wait for the party! It'll be so much fun!" Carolyn squealed. Of course it would be fun for her. She had a boyfriend AND a date.

"You have a boyfriend, and a date to the dance. I have zip. That doesn't look very fun to me," I sighed.

"It's Ok. You should go anyway. I'll stick with you." Carolyn hugged me.

"Fine," I sighed.

"See you there?" she looked me in the eye smiling.

"Yeah," I laughed and walked away.

AfTer ClaSs...
"Hello, Polly!" a voice said. I turned around.

"Hello. Who are you and how do you know my name?" I asked.

"Oh, my name is Skylar. I know all the names of the new college students. I like your necklace," he said.

"Thank you. A friend got it for me a while ago. It's a-,"

"Ring that doesn't fit you finger anymore. That happens," he said smiling.

"Can you, like, not talk to me." I asked.

"But don't you want to talk."

"Not to you. No."

"There are no such things as strangers. Only friends you haven't met yet."

"Ok. Get away please! You're scaring me",

"You're going to get kicked off the team with that attitude, Polly Brooks." He stopped. I stopped. He's not. He couldn't be. Is he? Impossible! I thought.

"What team? I'm not on any teams," I asked suspiciously. Ok, this next part is totally predictable. I know, but I would have never thought this would've happened till after it did. It wasn't predictable to me.

"Oh, you quit baseball after your friend moved?" he said.

"Baseball? I haven't been played baseball since I was, like, nine," I said.

"You haven't? Well, that's a shame. You sure were good at it," he smiled.

"Skylar?" I asked turning around, "Coach Skylar?"

"You remember!" He smiled.

I ran up and hugged him.

"I haven't seen you in so long!" I said.

"Yeah. I know."

"I'm glad you're here. You've changed so much. I have no friends besides Carolyn especially since Icky Nicky is here."

"Delightful. She's still around." Skylar smiled again.

"Unfortunately. Why does she have to hate ME? Of all people she hates me," I sighed.

"How would I know? I never met the girl."

"We are seeing each other for the first time in years. Years! And the first thing we talk about is Icky Nicky. I hate Icky Nicky and she becomes the center of my conversation. I'd expect us to be like 'Hey how's life going? What's been happening?" I pulled some gum out of my backpack and slipped it into my mouth.

"Are you going to the party?" he smiled.

"Not with anyone." I blushed.

"Would you like to go with me?" he looked at me.

"I'd like that."

Soon we arrived at my dorm and I said good-bye before going to pick out an outfit for the party. I hummed my favorite song and danced around the room.

"Skylar is here!" I told Carolyn.

"Isn't he the one you fell in love with?" Carolyn asked smiling.

"I never said I loved him, but I know I like him." I knew Carolyn knew everything.

ThAt NigHt...

"You look great!" Skylar smiled. I was wearing a short red dress and had put a slight bounce into my hair. I looked better than I had any other day.

"Let's go." I smiled taking his hand.

"I saw you watching me last year at the New York City Public Library. Why were you doing that?" I asked remembering the moment.

"Actually, Polly, I've never been to that library." His face fell.

"But I saw you there." I got a little worried.

"I wasn't the one you saw," he sighed as we turned the corner of the hallway.

"I was." A man was right there in front of us with an evil smirk on his face.

"Who are you?" I shivered stepping back. Skylar was glaring at him.

"Why don't you recognize your own father?" he asked.

"Get away from her!" Skylar stepped in front of me.

"Oh my God! Skylar he's going to kill me!" I cried.

"I just want to," my father pulled out a gun and held it towards Skylar, "Say hello."

"I'm sorry, sir, but I can't let you do that." Skylar stepped forward. He somehow got the gun out of the man- um; my father's- hand and it flew to the side.

They fought, but eventually Skylar got him down. My father looked like he couldn't move. He crawled to the end of the hall and went unconscious. Skylar saw me crying on the wall and ran to sit next to me. He hugged me tight and whispered in my ear that everything would be ok and he would call security. I nodded and slowly stopped crying. I touched my cheek to wipe off some blood he got on me when he hugged me. We laughed for no reason and I sniffled. This is a scary thing. I hope you haven't been that close to being murdered, but if you have, it's scary.

The guard picked up the gun and dragged my father away.

"Skylar?" I looked up at his face. It was all cut up.

"Yeah?" he asked.

"I...um..." I didn't know what to say. It was an awkward moment. I leaned forward and kissed him. It was silent and I was happy.

"Let's get you cleaned up," I said standing up and grasping his hand.

I took him back to his dorm where I tried my best to help with the cuts. We decided to go out for coffee instead of to the party. The night went well, and as I said, I was very, very happy. When I told Carolyn the story and how I knew Skylar, she was both excited and freaking out. I had to present my case in court with Skylar, because of the fact that people found a badly wounded convict with a gun close by in the hall that claimed to have met up with us. After a month, Skylar and me won the case. Carolyn and Mason were still together. We often went on double dates, and Skylar and Mason became good friends. It was probably one of the greatest times of my life.

CHAPTER**EIGHTEEN**

EaRly The nExt yeAr...

"**O**h my gosh!" Carolyn came running into our dorm yelling excitedly. I saved my story and closed the laptop while asking what it was that she was so excited over.

"Skylar told Mason who told me that...that..." She was breathless. And I could tell that she half wanted to tell me, but the other half knew she shouldn't.

"What is it?" I asked plopping down on my bed. This seemed important.

"I can't tell you. You'll find out and freak! You'll be so happy, but you have to wait," she smiled.

"Oh my gosh, Skylar said this?" I asked catching on to what it was.

"Yes. When he tells you to meet him in the cafeteria at sunset, look your best!" she bit her lip, as her grin grew deeper.

"I know what's going to happen!" I could barely help screaming at the top of my lungs.

"I know it's so awesome! I can't wait!" Carolyn sighed. We talked about it, but strangely, we never mentioned any plans or even what it actually was. It is usually hard to have a conversation without mention the subject of the conversation. Then Carolyn told me about a party that everyone on campus was going to. Everyone had been invited, but it was Icky Nicky's party. I didn't want to go at first, but then I figured if everyone is going and I had been invited to my worst enemy's party, I might as well go. Besides, I knew if I had been invited, then something must have been up and I wanted to find out what. Parties. They started to get on my nerves because every party or dance didn't turn out as amazing as I thought it would.

NeXt Day...

My cell phone rang while I was walking back to my dorm after my classes were over.

"Hello?" I asked without checking the caller ID. I was tired, and planned on napping for a while.

"Hey! Meet me at the cafeteria to see the sunset?" I smiled and sang a little song to myself.

"Sure. What for?" I asked as if I had no idea.

"If I told you, it wouldn't be a surprise, would it?"

"I guess not. I'll see you then. Love you." I hung up and stopped walking. Instead I ran to the dorm to meet Carolyn there.

"Ah!" I screamed excitedly.

"Sunset? Skylar? You? Today?" Carolyn jumped up from bed and her book bounced around as she sat up.

"Let's start getting ready!" I squealed. Girls do that kind of thing a lot when they're excited.

SunSet.

"It's almost sunset." Carolyn put the finishing touches of makeup on my face.

"I know! Should I go now?" I asked.

"Go, go, go!" Carolyn pushed me out the door. I

grasped the Polly and Skylar ring tight in my hands. By the time I reached the cafeteria doors I let it hang and let out the breath that I realized I'd been holding. I pushed open the doors and stopped. Tears filled my eyes.

I watched her kiss him.

"Skylar! How could you? And for her?" I gestured to Icky Nicky.

"Polly! It's not what you think!" Skylar ran towards me.

"Great surprise!" the tears came down my face. I tore of the necklace and threw it at him.

"Take the stupid thing." I ran off. He just stood there holding the necklace, and his eyes looked glassy. At that moment I didn't care. I just wanted to go back to my room and lay down.

When I got there, Carolyn was hopping excitedly, but her smile fell when I rounded the corner with tears instead of cheers.

"Polly! What happened?" She asked concerned as I breezed by her. I just lay in bed and cried till I fell asleep.

Then next morning, I woke up and forgot what I was crying about. After a few moments, I remembered and cried again. Then Carolyn woke up and I decided to talk to her. After I explained, she hugged me and tried to comfort me, but I didn't stop crying. I wouldn't leave my room except for classes. Carolyn brought me my meals and tried, but failed to convince me Skylar didn't do anything and it was Icky Nicky setting him up. She told me to go to Icky Nicky's party. She made me go. I'm not sure why I did.

At tHe parTy...

I sat in a corner near the refreshments. I was still

moping, but not crying. I had seen Skylar pass by twice, but he only took a glance at me once. I wondered why he was still even in college even though he was around 22 years old.

"Would you like to dance?" I turned my head to see a good-looking guy asking me to dance.

"Ok." I said taking his hand. The beginning was quick and fun, and even some of the slow dances were fun, but the ending wasn't so great.

We were slow dancing and he (who's name I found out was Rob) asked me to go out with him. I froze up unsure if I wanted to start dating again, but agreed.

A few weeks later, I found out Andy was coming to visit for two weeks. I had been on a few dates with Rob, but we weren't really, like, together. I could tell he liked me, but I didn't think I was ready yet. I needed to tell Andy all about everything!

AnDy's ArRivAl...

"Hi!" I ran and hugged Andy.

"Oh my gosh, it seems like ages since I last saw you!" Andy's voice was different. Mature and very different.

"Oh, and this is Carolyn and Atka." I introduced the two before I took Andy to the dorm. There wasn't must space so she slept on the couch. I told her all about everything. She had to give me a lot of hugs. She got along with Carolyn very well. Us three were like the three amigos. The three musketeers. The three unblind mice. We were best friends.

One day, we sat down for lunch, and Andy made me so mad, but she didn't know it.

"Polls? Can you introduce me to him?" She nodded her heads towards Skylar.

"That's Skylar," Carolyn whispered as I hung my head.

"I'm so sorry!" Andy practically freaked out.

"It's ok. You can like him. You can even date him if you want and I really don't care," I sighed. At that moment I figured that I really didn't care any more and that I would move on with my life, but there would always be that empty space deep in my heart. Kind of.

"I'd hate to accept that, Polls." Andy looked at me. Carolyn looked me in the eyes and read my exact feelings.

"No. It's seriously ok with her. She wasn't lying when she said she didn't care," Carolyn told Andy. Andy nodded and excused herself to talk to Skylar. Through the two weeks, they had a short fling, but then Andy dumped him near the end of her stay.

"I couldn't take it. No matter what I did the thought haunted my mind. The thought that this was Polly's ex and he cheated on her! So I got rid of him." I knew Andy wasn't lying.

Soon she left, but I was ok. I felt a lot better after her stay for some reason.

A FeW MonThs LatEr...

I've been together with a guy named Rob. Rob wasn't the one I really loved. You could've considered him a backup boyfriend or that I was using him, but that's not true.

"You do know you don't have to date Rob." Carolyn looked at me. She always knew everything.

"I know."

"The year is almost over. After this year, it's one more year! Then we'll all be splitting up and making our ways into the cold cruel world. You can't start it by pretending to be happy and in love with someone you're not," she sighed.

"I know. I know. I know all his, but still, I don't know."

"I thought you said you knew?" Carolyn chuckled.

"What am I going to do with my life?"

"That's something only you can decide."

"You're always so...like...mysterious." I giggled a tiny bit.

"So are you going to continue going out with him, or not?"

I thought about this and decided on yes, I would continue my relationship with Rob. Carolyn didn't seem so happy, but she didn't bother trying to change my mind. She tried that already.

CHAPTER**NINETEEN**

LasT dAy of SchOol...

"Wanna spend a week or two at my place this summer?" Rob asked as he twirled me around. I laughed a bit and said I'd find out if I could.

Carolyn didn't want me to be with Rob. She said it wasn't right for me. I told her that it was a risk I was going to take. I also told her that if the right choice came by, I would grab it no matter what.

"Polly, I thought you were mature enough to make the right decisions," Carolyn said.

"I am mature enough. I chose to be with Rob instead of Skylar because Skylar cheated on me and that's not right."

"But I have a feeling he wasn't cheating on you. I mean Icky Nicky is known to get people into those kinds of situations. Besides we both know Rob is not the best choice for you."

I thought for a second. I knew Rob wasn't the right one for me, but he loved me. I knew he was only the "backup," and Icky Nicky did do that kind of thing, but I also knew that it didn't look like Icky Nicky was messing things up and just faking it because then he would've broke free. I explained my thoughts to Carolyn, but she interrupted.

"But this guy saved your life. This guy loves you and I don't think you are in love with him. You don't love each other. With Rob you don't have any romance just that he loves you. Think about it," Carolyn said clearly mad at my decision. She walked away and shook her head.

I was extremely angry with myself and knew that if I dated Rob that would mean I had absolutely no self-respect, but, for some lame reason, that didn't change anything.

The bEginNing Of thE eNd of ColLege...

That summer had been a horrible summer. I went to Rob's house, but his parents had strict rules (he was still looking for houses). Carolyn wouldn't stop trying to convince me to get back together with Skylar and Little Sky got really annoying. He kept talking about girls and sports. Being 12 he was into that kind of stuff. I actually couldn't wait to return to school.

"Polly it seems like ages since I last spoke to you!" Rob said kissing me. It kind of was. After I went to his house, I had been avoiding all calls and e-mails from him because I was thinking about our relationship, but Rob wasn't one to ask, 'Why didn't you respond to any of my calls or e-mails?' so it was ok.

Later on I met up with Carolyn who decided not to bug me about Skylar, it being the first day back and all. Skylar had graduated the year before so I didn't see him.

"Mason told me that Skylar said it wasn't his fault and Icky Nicky started kissing him to make you break up and make your life miserable," Carolyn said as we walked back to our room.

"He's only saying that. It's not true," I sighed.

"What are you doing here?" Icky Nicky said.

"This is my room, freak," I said as I looked at Icky Nicky in my room.

"No it's mine. Now get out. The dork rooms are all the way down and to the right," Icky Nicky said plopping her stuff on the bed.

"You can't just take our room!" Carolyn said.

"This is my new room," she said unpacking.

"We never got new rooms. Ever," I told her.

"So what? They put pity on the dork and her friend."

I found one of the people who take care of room assignments. She took Carolyn to another room and I was stuck with Icky Nicky.

"I hate you," I said.

"I hate you, too," she said.

"Your life is going to turn out like crap," I told her.

"Go to hell, Brooks," she scowled

"Sorry, already been there," I smiled deviously.

"What?" she asked as I walked away from her.

A FeW mOntHs LatEr...

"Oh my gosh! How could you?" Carolyn shrieked when we were finally alone in my room.

"Polly, Polly, Polly, Polly. You can't do this to yourself",

"But I already did. I said yes to living with fake love." My voice cracked and I started to cry. I needed to hug her really tight. I told her I wanted to go home and start life all over again. She told me that the past already happened and I couldn't change it. She told me it was ok and from now on, I just had to think about things more and live every moment as if it was my last so I wouldn't mess up so bad.

"I hope everything turns out ok for you," Carolyn said.

"I hope so, too," I cried.

Icky Nicky walked in with her friends.

"I let you guys stay here alone for awhile. Now it's my turn," she said. I wiped off a tear and nodded. Carolyn took my hand and we walked out.

I was getting high grades and doing well with my book. I often went to stay with Carolyn and her new roommate. At least her roommate was nice, very unlike mine. The year ended and I graduated. My whole family came to my party, and Carolyn too. Her parents were too busy to throw her a party of her own. Mom nearly died when she found out I was engaged. She was happy for me. I guess she couldn't look into my eyes and tell my exact feelings like Carolyn could.

At the end of the party the most horrible thing happened. George had a heart attack. I cried and cried. So did Mom, Little Sky, Andy, Carolyn, and well, just about everyone, felt horrible. I felt like it was my fault, but at that time I had been feeling like everything was my fault. I walked away from the crowd around George and the ambulance. I sat in the bathroom and cried. After a while, I heard someone else crying. I sniffled and looked under the stall. Carolyn was in there crying too.

"I had to come in here because I couldn't stand it outside. I can't stand ambulances, you know? It's so sad. Polly I'm so sorry." I hugged her. I had to stop crying for Carolyn. Then I remembered something.

"Kind of crammed in here. Let's get out of here," I suggested. Carolyn nodded. When we got out, I needed to give people hugs, especially Mom. I was devastated and grateful for my loved ones all at once. Soon everyone left and I was alone with Little Sky and Andy.

Andy and I took a crying Little Sky back home. He went to his room.

"I can't believe you are getting married, and I'm not even dating. Even Little Sky has a girlfriend," Andy said.

"Don't rush it. Pick the right guy or else you'll ruin everything," I told her. I knew this from experience.

We had a beautiful funeral for George. Mom hadn't stopped crying for days, but at the funeral, her eyes were pretty much dried up from so much crying. She kissed his dead body before they shut the coffin. That was gross to me, but I wasn't about to tell my mom that. I cried a lot too. This guy was about the only real dad I'd ever had. My other dad tried to kill me. That's not very father like. George had had a good sense of humor. He was smart and always did the best for Little Sky and me or at least he tried to.

TiMe gOeS oN....

I moved in with Rob, and we had a baby boy. We named him Robby. I hadn't seen or heard from Skylar since college. I missed him and felt sorry for myself. Rob and I decided to wait before getting married. We didn't know when we said 'wait', that it meant 2 years.

CHAPTER**TWENTY**

TwO YeaRs laTer at StArbucks...

"**P**olly, when should we do the wedding?" Rob asked.

"As soon as possible," I smiled.

"How about August?" Rob flipped trough a wedding magazine looking at all types of stuff we could have at our wedding.

"Perfect. Oh, I love that!" I pointed to a white archway with white roses on it.

"Great!"

"Ok." Rob leaned in and gave me a kiss.

"Hi, Polly."

I looked up. Standing before me was Skylar.

"Hey, Skylar! I haven't seen you in years. How are you?" I tried to sound polite.

"Good. What about you? And Rob?"

"Good," Rob and I said at the same time.

"Do you mind if I borrow Polly for a sec? I need to talk to her about something. You can't hear because it's a surprise."

"Ok."

"Wait, Skylar, what...," Skylar grabbed my hand and took me outside.

"What did you want to talk to me about?" I asked.

"Seriously, Icky Nicky kissed me just because she saw you coming. I was about to push her away, but then she stood up and you declared you hated me." Skylar began.

"Oh, don't bring this up."

"But it wasn't me I swear",

"Yeah, right."

"No, really",

"Skylar, you were one of the only 3 people I trusted so much that I told you every single detail of my life every single secret I had and then you just went and turned on me like that."

"But it wasn't-"

"I heard enough Skylar. I'm going back inside to talk to somebody who cares about me."

"But, Polly, you can't marry Rob."

"Why? Give me one good reason."

"What if I said that you and I have been best friends and have known each other for a long time and I really trust you? And Polly, I love you. I want to marry you, not Rob. I mean, I'm not talking about me marrying Rob I'm talking about you marrying him, you know what I mean."

I loved Skylar, but I didn't know if I should give him another chance.

"Skylar, I...I... I have to go, Skylar. It's too late." I was going to cry. It was Icky Nicky trying to ruin my life the whole time. Not Skylar. And it worked. Icky Nicky did ruin part of my life. What was I supposed to say to Rob? "The only thing is it's too late and that's my fault."

"How is it too late?" Skylar asked.

"Because I'm engaged and-"

"Can't you get, like, break it off?"

"Skylar. You have to go."

"Polly!" Rob said. I turned around. "We have to go back to the house. Jenny said that Robby is starting to walk".

"Really? I'll be right there!" I was so excited. I turned back to Skylar, but my face fell.

"Robby is our son. Jenny is the babysitter," I said quietly.

"Ok," Skylar said. He looked so sad.

"Bye," I sighed.

"Here. Call sometime." Skylar pulled a piece of paper out of his pocket and scribbled something onto it. Then he handed it to me. It had his phone number on it. I just stared at it thinking why would he give me his number?

At HoMe...

"Robby, come to Mommy!" I knelt down far in front of Robby. He stumbled along until he fell down and landed in my arms. I laughed. Rob leaned down and kissed Robby and me.

"Listen, Polly, my boss says I have to work Saturday nights now too."

"Oh, Rob, you work all the time. When will you have time for us?" I picked up Robby and stood up.

"Saturday during the day and Sundays all day and all night. I'm also off all holidays too."

"But, Honey, that's just not enough," I said.

"I'm sorry," Rob said.

"I'll get it," I said to the ringing telephone.

"Hi Polly! It's Skylar. You probably don't want to talk to me, but if it's ok. Can we just be friends? I was wondering if you and Andy, Carolyn, Little Sky, and even Robby wanted to come for dinner or something."

"Um." I began. "How about Saturday night?"

"Good."

"I'll call everyone."

"Ok. Bye Polly."

"Bye."

I called Andy. She was going to Atlantic City with her friend. I called my brother. He was doing stuff with his friends. Carolyn had to work. Then I called Skylar to tell him I could meet him. We decided on Frank's Steak House. We acted like nothing was wrong, but I didn't know how much longer I could pretend.

SaTurDay NigHt...

"Bye, Honey!" I said kissing Rob.

"I'm not leaving yet."

"Robby and I are going for dinner with some old friends. I love you. Call my cell if you need me."

"Ok. Bye."

I drove to Frank's. Inside, Skylar was sitting at a table waiting for us.

We had lots of fun talking at dinner. Friendly talking. Then it started to get late.

"I should go now."

"All right. See ya, Polls",

"Bye, Skylar."

I hugged him and walked away. There was a couple at the table next to us kissing. I noticed this because one of them looked like Rob.

"Rob?" I asked. He turned around and stood up quickly.

"Polly! Hi! I didn't know you'd be here at Frank's tonight!" he said forcing a smile.

"You two-timed me?" My eyes filled with tears. I slapped him across the face. He tried to convince me he wasn't, but he stumbled with his words.

"Here's is your ring." I took off my ring and threw it at his eye, "We're OVER!" Geez. I mean seriously. I was using this guy as my backup guy and he cheated like the first one supposedly did. I'm not even sure why I cried if I didn't love him. It's a cruel thought, but slapping him was so much fun. Even if it probably didn't hurt him.

"Wait! Polly! It wasn't my fault."

"Don't mess with my friend! Polly has been through a lot of hurt and you didn't make it any better!" Skylar said. He ran after me.

"Polly!" Skylar yelled. I hugged him and cried. Robby cried too, but only because I was crying and he didn't know what was going on.

"It'll be all right Polly. I'll drive you home." We hopped into my car and he drove me to my house.

"I'll help you collect your stuff," Skylar said. We walked into the house and I packed my things. Then we went back outside as I thought where could I go.

"Thank you, Skylar," I smiled, "I think I'm gonna stay with my mom for a while. Just till things straighten out."

"Polly? Can I ask you something?"

"Yes?"

"Polly Brooks," Skylar took the Polly-Skylar ring out of his pocket and I was like totally freaking out, but I was perfectly sure not to show it. "Will you," he went down on his knees.

"Oh, God yes!" I said, grabbing the ring before he could finish. I kissed him and we just stayed standing there for a few moments, forgetting about my stuff, Baby Robby, Rob, and everything else.

CHAPTER**TWENTY-ONE**

7 yEarS laTer...

"**H**appy Birthday Dear Marie, Happy Birthday to You!" We sang happily to our daughter.

"How old are you now, Marie?" I asked.

"I'm 5!" She laughed.

"Wow! You're getting really big! Stop growing up so fast, Marie!" Skylar said picking her up kissing her on the check. She laughed.

"Mommy why is it raining on my birthday? Is God sad?" Marie looked at me. It was pouring rain outside.

"No. He's crying because he's happy! We're all together one big happy family." The doorbell rang.

"Amy's here!" Marie jumped up and down as she ran to the door. It was Andy, my mom, Little Sky, his fiancée, Carolyn, Mason, and their daughter Amy.

"Mommy! Daddy! Look who's here!" Marie was so happy. She went to play Barbie with Amy and I smiled remembering how I did that all the time with Andy, who smiled too.

LatEr tHat nighT...

"Marie, do you want to come outside with me?" I

asked. Everyone had left and now it was just our family.

"But Mommy it's raining," Marie sighed.

"That doesn't mean we can't play outside!" I said. Marie and I went outside.

"Sing a song Marie so we can dance," I said twirling her around.

"I know a song! Twinkle twinkle little star!" Marie started to sing. Of course I sang with her.

"How I wonder what you are!" I laughed.

As we danced through the rain, my daughter and I, I became deep in thought. My mission was something I was never told, but my mission was complete. The Devil wasn't the one who sent me on the mission. It was God. And as I watch those rain drops fall to this very day, I know that God gave me what I wanted, but it wasn't anything on my list. I had a great life, but I didn't need fame and fortune. All I needed was love, care, family, friends, and a little help from my friend God.

The End

Did you enjoy the book?
Is there anything you'd like to change?
If so, go to www.MackenzieLowry.webs.com
and be a part of "POLLYWOOD the Fan Edition"!

Acknowledgements

Carolyn Etienne is one of my best friends and extremely trustworthy. She can read my mind and helped a lot with this book. She was also very supportive. She had sneak previews and read parts of it. I love her very much!

Mom & Dad are the best parents ever and very supportive of this book. They helped with the editing too. I want to thank them for always being there for me and taking such good care of my brother and me. We are a gift and a curse to them (Monk). They are a just a gift to me. They are also the cooliest.

All my Aunts, Uncles, Cousins, and my Grandparents, also Mariel and Especially my Grandpa are so crazy, but I love them and they all wanted to read this book. I didn't tell any of them what it was about, to save it as a surprise. I love 'yous' always and forever! Psst... Kream Cheese Kuzlins Together Forever!

My Annoying Friends who I love even though they are all weird 'in their own special way' (words of Sarah). They all wanted read my book, but I wouldn't let them. They were all supportive and many of my characters in the book were modeled after my friends. They are all here in my book and in my heart.

All my Teachers who helped me a lot, and without them I couldn't have written this book.

I Love You All!

Printed in the United States
203124BV00002B/1-180/P

9 781432 720544